BETTE DAVIS

Also by Roy Moseley

My Stars and Other Friends
Merle: The biography of Merle Oberon (with Charles Higham)
Roger Moore: A Biography (with Philip & Martin Masheter)
Rex Harrison: The First Biography (with Philip & Martin Masheter)
Cary Grant: The Lonely Heart (with Charles Higham)
A Life With The Stars

BETTE DAVIS

An Intimate Memoir

Roy Moseley

Sidgwick & Jackson
LONDON

To my Mother and Father
and Bette Davis, who
liked each other.
And for Mitch Douglas.

First published in Great Britain in 1989
by Sidgwick & Jackson Limited
1 Tavistock Chambers, Bloomsbury Way
London WC1A 2SG

ISBN 0 283 99866 0
Phototypeset by Input Typesetting Ltd, London
Printed by Mackays of Chatham Plc, Chatham, Kent

Contents

Preface

Bette Davis was one of my best friends. Nobody could have had a better friend. For years I believe I knew her as well as anybody except her close family – her daughter B.D., her son-in-law Jeremy, and Michael Merrill, the son Bette adopted when she was married to the actor Gary Merrill. The Merrills' adopted daughter Margot was brain damaged, but she certainly 'knew' her mother. There was also Robin Brown, Bette's neighbour in Westport, Connecticut, where much of my story takes place, who has known Bette from the time they were both at drama school together.

Bette's charming cousins, John and Sally Favor of Laguna in California also knew her well, as did Grace Brynolson and Ellen Batchelder, her friend from schooldays. Peggy Shannon and Vik Greenfield both worked closely with Bette during the time that I knew her, as did her lawyer Harold Schiff. And Bette's sister Barbara and her family probably knew her best of all.

Throughout my friendship with Bette Davis I met all those lovely people, except Barbara, and we shared our affection for her, our admiration for her, and our worries about her.

So how do we choose our friends? Why did she choose me? That is a question I am always being asked. The next question people ask is 'What was she like?' I do not believe that any other celebrated person interests people and excites their imagination quite as much as this greatest of movie stars.

During some parts of our friendship I don't believe that even the people I have named above were as close to her as I was. Now, like many of her friends, I must talk of Bette in the past tense, as we have all shared the common fate of being expelled from her friendship and from her life. I miss her very much. So now I have written the story of Bette and Roy, to explain how it happened that Roy Moseley, a public-school-educated Englishman half her age, found his 'Auntie Mame', the greatest star of them all. I want to tell you what she was like.

1

The Beginning of a Beautiful Friendship

The seeds of my admiration for Bette Davis were first sown at The Cinema in Guildford, Surrey. Guildford is a prosperous English cathedral town, thirty miles south of London. Full of neat houses, set amongst rolling green hills, it is a long way from the glamour of Hollywood. I was an only child and, like most only sons, I was extremely close to my mother, who was a strong and beautiful woman. I adored her and allowed her to help in shaping many of my tastes and interests. She was also my best friend. It was she who first introduced me to Bette Davis's films, and it was like a new world opening up to me.

I have found in my life that there are certain moments to be had in the theatre or cinema which lift the spirits of a person so high that the experience is virtually immaculate. I have been fortunate enough to have had a few of these moments. I saw Judy Garland on stage, and Nureyev and Fonteyn dancing in the fifth performance of their *Romeo and Juliet*. There was Maria Callas in *Norma* and Olivier in many things. There were a few others, and there were the performances of Bette Davis. Everything about the woman I saw on the screen was larger than life and twice as exciting: the way she dressed, the way she moved, the way she spoke, the way she drank and the way she smoked. Every mannerism, expression and phrase seemed like magic to me. She epitomised all that life should be about. She was strong, stylish and dramatic. I liked everything about her. She seemed to be talking directly to me, to be mirroring my thoughts, my needs and my ambitions.

The pictures in which Bette appeared were pure Hollywood. The best ones were classics, containing moments which are still more vivid in my memory than many things which have happened to me in life. Even in the bad ones Bette Davis was always spellbinding. Most of her characters have become as real in my memory

1

as flesh and blood. I remember their names and almost everything that happened to them. She made them alive.

At school I would regale my friends with the plots of every film, telling the story in a voice which I thought was a deadly accurate impersonation of Bette Davis's. She had a way of pouncing on an unexpected word in a sentence which would lift it up out of a script, and make the words ring in the listener's ears. It was music to me. But how could a young boy living in a suburban town in Britain hope to meet such a great star? I might just as well have been hoping to become a confidante of the Queen of England. Apart from anything else I was still a fumbling schoolboy, while she was a mature woman, at the height of her power.

At times it seemed like a hopeless dream but at other times, when I felt strong, determined and awash with youthful optimism, I swore to myself that I would get there. I didn't know how, and I could not have explained to anyone else why this was not a laughable ambition, but I just knew it had to be. All my life I have been a fighter. Few have ever opened any doors for me. I have had to push them open for myself, and I knew that Bette Davis was the same. She was not born with a silver spoon in her mouth but had fought all the way through her career, and it was this strength which attracted me.

As a young girl Bette was taken by her mother to audition for Eva LeGallienne in New York. Miss LeGallienne was a great actress who took on a certain number of pupils and trained them with a rigorousness which meant only the toughest survived. Bette wanted to be accepted by her more than anything, but the interview turned out to be a humiliating experience. Bette was questioned about the books she had read and asked to recite a speech by an ancient Dutch woman in a Dutch accent. Miss LeGallienne obviously had no interest in this unimpressive-looking child and took no trouble to hide her contempt. She told Bette that she was a frivolous little girl, and suggested she go away and raise a family because she would never be an actress.

This sort of rejection is what distinguishes the winners from the losers. The losers take the advice they are given and relinquish their ambitions, melting back into the anonymous crowd. The eventual winners take each piece of discouragement as a personal insult and set out with even more determination to prove their detractors are wrong. This is how Bette reacted to every set-back in her career, and gradually this determination led to her emerging from the crowd and, eventually, to her becoming the greatest film star ever. My own ambitions had received similar discouragement from many people but I always knew what I wanted, and I always knew that eventually I would achieve it. Seeing how Bette had triumphed against the odds was an inspiration to me. It gave me hope for my own future and helped me to keep on battling against the odds.

Many years later I was at a party and I spotted Miss LeGallienne across the room. I went over to her and asked for an autograph, covering up the facing page in my book with a piece of paper. She signed for me and then I uncovered the other side of the page, showing an extravagant Bette Davis signature.

'Is it true,' I asked, 'that you told Bette Davis she would never be an actress?'

Miss LeGallienne was not amused, protesting that at that time she was seeing hundreds of hopeful young girls every day, so some were bound to slip through the net. All great success stories happen like this. They start with just one more face in the crowd, and perseverance and talent lift that face out and make it into something special. At The Cinema in Guildford I was just one more face in the audience, one amongst the millions of people all round the world who watched Bette Davis on the screen, but I was to be lifted out to become, for a while, one of her closest friends.

Bette's press coverage over the years gives a complex and contradictory picture. In the standard fan magazines she was reported to be living the typical film star life of nightclubs, parties and the Hollywood 'round'. Early in her career she had learned the art of giving interviewers what they wanted to hear, and what the studios wanted the public to believe. I was later to find out that she had little interest in the false, glittering side of Hollywood society, preferring to live a normal life at home and hungry to work whenever she could, as hard as she could. In later interviews, as her position as a big star became more assured, she began to rebel against the studios. She would give indiscreet quotes to reporters about the dangerous powers of the censor's office, and attended a Democratic rally in New York against the wishes of her studio in Hollywood. Then there had been her long and expensive legal battle against Warners, fought on British soil. She had tried to change the system which meant that film stars were virtually slaves, albeit well-paid ones, of the studios. She lost the fight and had to go back to Warners with her tail between her legs, but the stand she had taken eventually led to film stars gaining the freedom to have more choice of the work offered to them and, in many cases, to become very wealthy individuals. All this publicity showed me someone who was afraid of nothing, and who would do anything to ensure that her work was of the highest standard possible.

As I grew into adolescence, I began to learn that it was not impossible to meet the objects of my fantasies in the flesh. I learned how to find out when and where the great stars would be appearing. I knew where to meet them as they flew in to British airports on tours to promote films or biographies. However much I admired them on the screen, I discovered that I was not afraid to walk up and talk to any of them in the flesh, as most other people seem to be. I found many of them to be exceptionally friendly and accessible people. I realised that they actually were just people like the rest of us, and that there was no reason why I could not become their friend, given the right circumstances – and luck. They were not, as the studios would have us believe, gods and goddesses. They might look more glamorous than the rest of us, and they might live differently, but inside they were the same. They were sometimes happy and sometimes unhappy, sometimes pleasant and sometimes nasty. They too could be lonely and in need of friendship and love, often even more than the rest of us. My ambitions grew stronger. I was never afraid to step out of the crowd and introduce myself to my idols. Sometimes I would meet with initial rejection, but that didn't worry me. Most of the time I found that they wanted to meet people who had the courage to come forward. Over a period of a few years I met most of the famous figures who populated my internal world, with one exception – Bette Davis. She seldom came to England at that time.

Upon leaving school I followed my dreams into the world of showbusiness. Having no talent to perform myself, I looked for every possible backdoor into the profession. I worked as a dresser, apprentice impresario and finally agent, in order to enter the mysterious and tempting world of films and theatre. Everything that I found behind the proscenium arch and behind the cinema screens lived up to my fantasies, but still one thing eluded me. No-one seemed able to help me to meet Bette Davis. The harder a prize is to obtain the more people will value it. The more elusive

Bette Davis became the more my burning desire to meet her was fuelled.

Finally my chance arrived in 1958. Miss Davis was due to arrive in England to film *The Scapegoat* with Alec Guinness. She was flying in from Rome, where she had been on a much publicised sightseeing trip and had visited the set of *Ben Hur*, which was being directed by her friend and favourite director, William Wyler. I found out which flight she would be on and when it would be landing at Heathrow, and I set out for the airport hours before the plane was due to arrive.

I knew where to go in the bustle and crush of the airport in order to ensure that stars and other VIPs did not slip past me on their way into the country, and I settled down to wait. As the time of arrival approached other people began to join me. Photographers and reporters started gathering around. The arrival of such a legend on British shores was a major news story and media excitement was undoubtedly being further fuelled by the publicity people involved with the film. The crowd became larger and I had to jostle and push to ensure that I stayed near the front. Every minute seemed like an eternity as we waited for the doors to swing open and the great lady to stride out.

Suddenly she was there, surrounded by eager-eyed officials from the airline. The crowd surged forward begging for signatures, pictures and quotes. She moved fast, just as I knew she would, walking with that swagger which I had watched so many times on the screen, her shoulders pulled back and her head held high. My heart was pounding as I pushed forward to be close to her.

She was exactly as I had imagined her to be: a magnetic, powerful figure holding the whole crowd in thrall. She had put on a little weight at the time, but her legs were still as young and shapely as they had been when she first struggled her way from Broadway to Hollywood all those years before. She strode out towards us with the familiar swing of the hips. She was dressed in dramatic, dark colours, complete with gloves, which were part of her formal wardrobe, and hat. From the hat a veil was draped, and through the black netting I could see the famous features. There were the glaring eyes, which she could flash so fiercely when she chose that they seemed almost to jump from their sockets. Her mouth was the same, seemingly giant, gash of lipstick through which I had heard her so often spitting out her lines on the screen.

She commanded the crowd to fall back and I found myself close enough to touch her.

'I will sit here and I will answer your questions!' she told the crowd.

She sat, placing a massive airport ashtray on her lap. She pulled out a cigarette with a characteristic flourish and placed it surely between her lips, as if the veil did not exist. I was later to discover that this was simply instinctive. The style of it all took my breath away. She fielded questions from the reporters and posed for the photographers like a true professional. She knew what they were there to get and she gave it to them, as she had been doing for over thirty years by then. For me it was a great experience to watch this professional at work – for this really was Bette Davis working.

As always happens at these events when they occur spontaneously in public places, other onlookers had begun to gather to see what all the fuss was about. The crowd was swelling but Miss Davis was still in command. I have often noticed that when members of the public are viewing a celebrity from close quarters, they tend to talk about them in loud tones as if they were not people, with real feelings that can be hurt. Perhaps they think that they are like their images on the screen, distant and deaf to anything the audience might say.

Across the general babble of noise one woman's voice carried clearly to all our ears: 'Doesn't she look old?'

I felt a hot rush of anger surging through me. How could anyone be so rude and ignorant? Unable to control myself I shouted back across the crowd: 'Have you looked in a mirror recently, madam?'

My outburst took the crowd by surprise and everyone went quiet for a moment. The eyes behind the veil turned to look at me and the lips mouthed a word of thanks. She stretched out a gloved hand and squeezed my fingers.

Within minutes the press conference was over and she had disappeared, whisked away by minders to a waiting limousine somewhere outside a well-guarded security door. The crowd dispersed and I was left, having realised an ambition. I had seen Bette Davis. I had actually touched her, but now it was all over and she had gone. I knew that was not going to be enough to satisfy me. Seeing her I knew that she would never be a disappointment to me, as many film stars can be when you meet them in the flesh.

She was just as much of a legend in a crowded and brightly lit airport arrival hall as she was on the screen. In the cinema she had had all the skills of the lighting cameramen, make-up and hairdressing departments to ensure that she was larger than life. At Heathrow she had had only her own personality and the reputation built up over the decades. I had to find other ways to meet Bette Davis.

Many years later, in his excellent biography of Bette Davis, Charles Higham was to quote the actress Jill Bennett, who was another admirer of the Bette Davis style:

> Bette told me 'Never see your rushes. You'll get depressed about how you look and you won't be able to do a thing about it.' I always hated the way I looked on the screen. Bette did too. I didn't need any encouragement not to see the rushes. I loved Bette. She was real, gutsy and very dangerous. Dangerous the way a star should be, and she told me something wonderful. She told me, 'Always make love to your props. To the furniture.' I told her I remembered the wonderful moment in *The Little Foxes* when she leaned against the door as though she wanted to kiss it. I often found myself making love to tea trays in pictures after that.
>
> One weekend, I had lunch with her at Grosvenor House. I bought her some yellow roses. She was waiting for me outside the elevator. No other star would do that. One night, we went to the greyhound races. She was got up tremendously for the occasion. She looked at me and said, 'You look awful. Why are you dressed like that?' I had a plain linen dress on. It was summer. I think a Mary Quant. She said, 'You won't be a star if you don't look like one.' She was in sequins and she said, 'I can't go into the races with you looking like this. You'll have to walk behind me as if you're my secretary.' And I did. It didn't bother me at all.

As Jill Bennett said, Bette Davis was real, gutsy and dangerous.

2

Dinner at White City

The one time I ever lied to any of my early employers was in order to see my idol in the flesh again. In 1961 *Whatever Happened to Baby Jane* was playing at the Warner Cinema in London's Leicester Square, and I spotted a tiny classified advertisement in the *London Evening Standard* announcing that Bette Davis would be there at eight thirty the following night. At the time I was working for the impresario Bernard Delfont. It was a job I was devoted to and normally I would never have done anything to endanger it, but I could not resist this opportunity to see Bette Davis again. I told my boss I had an appointment with the dentist, and left, guiltily, for the afternoon.

Feeling certain that I would not have been the only one to have seen the advertisement, I got to the cinema at two in the afternoon. I secured a front seat and just stayed there, watching the film go round and round while waiting to see her.

Baby Jane is a claustrophobic story about two former child actresses living in Hollywood in their late middle age. Bette was playing the title role in grotesque make-up, wig and costume, like a monstrous parody of Shirley Temple. Joan Crawford played her bed-ridden sister, whom Bette cruelly tortures, serving her a dead rat for breakfast and other ghoulish treats. The whole film is a pantomine of horror, made into a commercial success by two great performances from the stars.

Long before Bette was due to arrive, the cinema began to fill up. My mother and her aunt arrived a few hours later, and managed to squeeze into the back of the cinema before they closed the doors and started turning people away. Outside in Leicester Square the crowd control police had arrived, barriers were being erected and hundreds of people were gathering. It was like Oscar Night in Hollywood, all because of one small advertisement hidden in the middle pages of a paper. This was the sort of adulation that Bette

8

Davis could command. Everywhere she went vast crowds would form.

Exactly on cue Bette Davis walked through the audience and climbed onto the stage in front of the screen. She was accompanied by her daughter B.D., who was fifteen but towered a good seven inches over her tiny mother. The audience whooped with joy. Together they proceeded to give an impromptu act, including the song 'I've written a letter to Daddy, (who resides in heaven above)', which came from the film. As she finished singing she threw an envelope to her dead father up into the air in an hilarious gesture.

Just as suddenly she reverted to the tough, no-nonsense Yankee Dame, telling us all that somewhere in the auditorium, under one of the seats, was a numbered ticket. Whoever had the ticket would win a lifesize Baby Jane Doll as a prize. We all leapt up and began searching desperately. The unmistakeable voice cracked out above us from the stage.

'Never before have I seen so many asses at one time!'

As I became more established and successful in my career, my network of contacts broadened. I asked the same questions of everyone I met. Had they ever met Bette Davis? Could they introduce me to her? Some of them, of course, had met her in the course of their working lives, but none of them had managed to get close to her; all of them had stories to tell. Some of the stories illustrated how hard she worked and what a great craftswoman she was; others told of how monstrous she could be to people who displeased her. Everyone had favourite anecdotes about her. Some of them might have been based on truth, but all of them contributed to the reputation which this lady carried around with her of being 'real, gutsy and dangerous'.

As the years passed I seemed to be no nearer to my goal, and I began to wonder if I would ever get any closer to her than I had been at Heathrow. I became an agent and many of my famous clients, such as Jane Wyman and Olivia de Havilland, were American, so I began to be able to travel across the Atlantic regularly. Arriving in America, particularly Los Angeles and New York, was a dream come true for me. America was the country that made most of the films which I had watched and lived with so vividly for so many years. London seemed grey and dismal compared to the gloss and glamour of New York and the sunshine and beauty of Hollywood.

To me everyone in Hollywood seemed beautiful. At every party and in every restaurant I met the people I had been watching on the screen since I was a child, and few of them disappointed me. It seemed like a land of milk and honey, full of unlimited possibilities for an ambitious young man. I was meeting some of the biggest names in the world, stars who would be recognised anywhere they went, and who had amassed vast fortunes from their talents. I visited their homes in Beverly Hills, Bel Air and in Hollywood, I wined and dined and lounged by their pools with them, and every introduction seemed to open more doors and lead to more people.

But where was Bette Davis? Was she not the queen of Hollywood? Was she not the greatest star of them all? Why was she never at the dinner or cocktail parties, never at the first nights or press receptions? It was mystifying and tantalising.

I finally managed to make contact with a lady called Violla Rubber, who was Bette Davis's personal manager at the time and had been for several years. She was a stumpy, elderly and strong woman, but as long as she represented a possible path to Miss Davis I was willing to do anything for her. I later discovered that Miss Rubber had previously worked for Marlene Dietrich and Diana Barrymore, but was now devoted to Miss Davis, who bullied her mercilessly and continuously. Violla had also been a stage producer, involved in the Broadway production of Tennessee Williams' play *Night of the Iguana* which Bette had starred in. Miss Rubber wasn't the only woman who was besotted by Bette Davis. Every day that Miss Davis worked at Warners Studios, Marlene Dietrich had a single white rose delivered to her dressing room – so I was told!

A famous lawyer friend of mine, who was travelling to America with me, told me that Bette liked to meet new people, and that she also liked the English. I felt encouraged and we tried to set up a meeting. Finally, during one of my visits to the United States, Miss Rubber said she thought Miss Davis would meet me in Connecticut. I flew from Los Angeles to New York for the promised meeting only to find once more that it was not to be. I returned to England feeling that perhaps it just wasn't meant to be.

Sometimes you can do everything in your power to achieve a particular goal and still fail, and then some small acts of fate, going on behind the scenes, conspire to bring about the result which you have been fighting to achieve. When Bette Davis arrived in Cannes in 1961 to promote *Baby Jane* at the film festival, she still had her fifteen-year-old daughter B.D. with her. During the festival many of the biggest names in the world of films fly in to promote their latest products. Every hotel is full and the rich and famous often have to stay on the luxury yachts which are moored in the blue sea off the beach, just to be sure of getting a bed – and of escaping the paparazzi at the end of each working day. Although they are ostensibly there to see and judge films, they spend most of the time socialising and making deals. It is one vast round of highly publicised parties and meetings. A young girl, especially the daughter of one of the most famous film stars in the world, needed to have an escort to take her to the various functions.

Miss Davis asked The Seven Arts publicity office to arrange for someone to accompany B.D., and they came up with a young man called Jeremy Hyman. Jeremy's mother Dorothy Hyman had a sister who had, co-incidentally, married another man with the same surname – Elliott Hyman. Elliott was President of Seven Arts Films, the company which Jeremy was working for at the time, and which had produced *Baby Jane*.

B.D. was a nice, if statuesque, girl with a pretty face, but she did not have her mother's glamour. She was very tall and very busty. Although he was nearly twice the girl's age, Jeremy agreed to look after her, seeing it as a corporate duty more than a pleasure. B.D. could have expected to be confronted with a bald, fat, cigar-smoking film executive, which was what her mother had hoped for. Instead, to Miss Davis's horror, Jeremy proved to be extremely attractive and proceeded to sweep B.D. off her feet. The couple fell in love at first sight and Miss Davis quickly realised that she was in danger of losing her daughter to a man who didn't seem to be the least bit impressed by the great Bette Davis. She was beside herself with anxiety and anger and did everything she could to part them.

Perhaps she had hoped that she and B.D. would be together for as long as she and her own mother had been. Ruthie had virtually lived out her own life through her daughter Bette. At film pre-mières, for instance, it would be Ruthie who would walk in ahead of Bette, and Ruthie who had the more glamorous dress. Bette had never questioned this, and had never resented anything that Ruthie had done since she believed that her success was entirely due in the first instance to her mother's faith in her abilities and self-sacrifices. She had obviously hoped for the same sort of selfless devotion from B.D. but unfortunately B.D. had other plans, which didn't include being part of a Hollywood star's entourage all her life – even if that star was her mother.

The heady atmosphere of the Riviera festival was the perfect setting for romance. As B.D. explained in her book, she suddenly found herself to be one of the 'beautiful people', and it was a wonderful experience. When she and Jeremy announced that they planned to marry, despite B.D.'s youth, Miss Davis was apoplectic. She rushed B.D. away from Cannes, driving up through France with Violla Rubber, but she just wasn't able to keep the determined young girl and her suitor apart. She later told me that on arriving in London, where she was staying at the Mayfair Hotel, she laid all her jewellery out on the bed and prepared to commit suicide. She then caught sight of herself in the mirror and burst out laughing.

She was certain that, based on her own unfortunate experiences, all men were 'bastards' and that this 'English bastard' was the worst of the lot. She tried every trick in the book to put her beloved B.D. off, but her daughter was a chip off the old block when it came to grit and determination. Miss Davis then did everything she could think of to stop the marriage, but the two young lovers proved to be even more single-minded. Eventually she decided that there was nothing she could do but allow B.D. to learn from her own mistakes and she consented to them marrying.

The story reached me in England, and I could hardly believe my luck. I knew Jeremy Hyman! His family and mine had been friends. It shows how hopeless my position appeared to be at that stage that this tenuous, even negative link to Bette Davis seemed like a major breakthrough. She might not like Jeremy, but at least he was her son-in-law, and he was part of her family. I hadn't seen him for years, so I decided to renew the acquaintance and see what developed. I went to his office in New York to meet him, and reminded him of the long friendship between our parents. I then said that I would like to meet his new mother-in-law.

'You don't want to meet her,' he said.

'I assure you that I do.'

He cut me short. 'I wouldn't introduce anyone to that woman.'

I couldn't believe my ears. I was so offended that he should talk about Bette Davis like that, I could think of nothing to say in reply. Shaking with anger, I left the office. Although I later came to see more clearly the problems that Jeremy had to put up with from his mother-in-law, I always felt that he dealt with people in a high-handed and arrogant manner. When it came to looking after his wife, however, he could not be faulted – except by Miss Davis.

So that door was slammed shut before it had even opened. I did feel, however, that I was edging closer to my prey. Fate was also working on my case in another area. Some years later, quite by accident, I became involved in a book called *The Death of a President* by William Manchester. I was instrumental in producing a recording of it for the blind, to be donated to the library at the Kennedy Centre in Washington DC. Miss Davis has always been an avid Democrat and particularly worshipped John F. Kennedy. Anyone who did anything even vaguely connected with the family was all right with her. Violla Rubber happened to read about the work I was doing in an article in the *London Evening News* and finally, one magic day, she telephoned me and asked me to meet her at Fortnum and Mason's in Piccadilly.

'Bette Davis will be coming to London to make a film,' she told me, 'and she would like to meet you.'

Inside my head a little warning voice told me to be cautious. Miss Rubber had, after all, promised meetings before, but this time it seemed impossible that anything could go wrong. London was not such a big place as America. It would be much harder for the great Miss Davis to elude me here than it had been over there. I was on my home territory and she was the visitor, whereas over there I had no idea how to find her once she had gone to ground.

At last, in 1967, the meeting was set up at the White City dog track, a stadium in the bleaker part of West London, close to the BBC Television Centre. Miss Davis loved to go 'to the dogs' when she was in England and she had booked a large table in the restaurant overlooking the track, in order to entertain some friends. I was to join them for dinner.

13

The day before the dinner, I heard that Miss Davis had a cold, and that she was cancelling all social engagements. My heart sank, but I received no word about a cancellation, so I set out for West London, still not sure if she would be there or not. I remember so plainly walking into the restaurant and seeing her sitting at the end of the table. There was no hat and veil this time, although she was wearing gloves as she always did in public. This time we were not separated by a stage or by police barriers. There she was, my hostess for the evening. Roger Moore and his wife were also at the table, as were the producer Jimmy Sangster and the director Roy Ward Baker with their wives. The restaurant was full of celebrities but Miss Davis stood out from the crowd. She was obviously the most striking person in the room.

I could hardly take my eyes off her during the meal and when it came time to bet, she walked down the table and laid her hand on my shoulder. She showed me a small amount of dollars which she was holding in her other hand.

'Mr Moseley,' she said, 'this is Jeremy's money. So I think we should bet on something together.' Violla Rubber had, of course, told her about the Moseleys' friendship with the Hymans.

At another table in the restaurant my ex boss Bernard Delfont, one of Britain's most famous impresarios and the brother of film and television mogul Lew Grade, was also entertaining a party. After the meal I went over to his table and asked if he would like to meet Bette Davis. He said he would and I proudly took him over to Miss Davis and introduced him. He asked her if she would present 'The Delfont Cup' to the winner of the race which he sponsored and which was about to be run.

'I would be delighted,' she replied.

The crowd was stunned when it was announced that Bette Davis would be presenting the cup, and thousands of eyes were turned to the enclosure as she stepped out. She gave the winner his cup and then looked around at the other dogs and their trainers.

'Which one came in third?' she snapped.

'This one, Miss Davis,' said Mr Delfont, indicating a greyhound shivering in the middle of the line.

Striding over to the animal she administered a sharp clout to its nose with her hand. 'You!' she said to the dog, 'I had my money on you.' The crowd roared with laughter.

As we came to part I plucked up courage and asked if I might visit her on the set of *The Anniversary*, the film she was making at that time.

'Of course, Mr Moseley,' she said, 'phone me on Tuesday evening.'

She gave me her private telephone number. I was delighted and excited by the prospect of watching her work. She left the room so fast I hardly saw her go, and when I left the stadium that night I was walking on air. Finally we had met. She knew my name, and we were going to meet again. It was the culmination of a dream, and the start of a wonderful friendship.

3
The Chantry

Everywhere I go in the world I hear the name of Bette Davis. I hear her talked about on the top decks of London buses and in first-class cabins of jumbo jets. I see impersonations on the television screen and read articles in the press. The whole world finds her fascinating. She's not just a great actress, she is a star, a legend, an image, a mystery. The world wants to know about her. She is an industry in her own right, like the Ford Motor company or Pepsi Cola. Whenever she works she is insured for millions; whatever she does is watched by millions. Could it really be that someone so famous, so admired, could become my friend?

When the day arrived for my visit to the set I was as nervous as if the evening at White City had never happened. Although I knew that she was always approachable to the man in the street, I had heard hundreds of horror stories of how she behaved when she was working. I knew that she could be tyrannical if her concentration was disturbed. Would she really not mind being disturbed by me? Would she remember she had invited me? Would she remember me at all? All these thoughts were going through my mind as I headed out for Elstree Studios.

I needn't have worried for a moment. She was perfectly charming as she showed me over the set. *The Anniversary* was the story of a terrifying mother, played by Miss Davis. One of her sons is a transvestite, another an unhappy husband and the third a promiscuous lecher. Miss Davis had to wear an eye patch over her left eye, which gave her a great deal of discomfort and also set the tone for the rest of the melodramatic plot. It was being made by Hammer Productions, who specialised in low-grade horror movies.

Once shooting had broken for lunch we left the set together to have something to eat. Violla Rubber was also there, as was Miss Davis's beau at the time, a very boorish Englishman she had met on the liner over from America to Europe. During the lunchtime

16

conversation we started talking about Dorothy Parker, whose death had just been announced.

'I would love to have met Dorothy Parker,' I enthused.

'Perhaps,' grunted the surly boyfriend, 'but would she have wanted to meet you?'

I felt crushed, but Miss Davis leapt to my defence. 'I,' she snapped, 'am also very famous. A lot of people would like to meet me, and I would like to meet all of them, so that I can make up my own mind which of them I like and which I don't – and they can decide whether they like me or not.'

The boyfriend did not speak again, and I stared hard at Violla Rubber to see if she was listening to these words. Miss Rubber stared impassively back and something told me, even then, that she was going to turn out to be an enemy. At that stage, however, she was proving to be extremely useful.

A few days after our lunch Miss Rubber telephoned me at my office. She started by asking if I knew of a good lawyer Miss Davis could use. I recommended David Jacobs, who I was very close to and who I had actually introduced to Brian Epstein, which had led to David working for the Beatles. Apparently Miss Davis wanted to be ready with a top lawyer should she need one. Miss Rubber then explained that she was going back to America and she asked if I would be good enough to 'look after' Miss Davis for her for as long as she was in England working on the film.

My breath was taken away, but I eventually managed to say, 'Lovingly, Miss Rubber, lovingly.'

Miss Davis's voice instantly came on the line. 'Thank you, Mr Moseley,' she said, and hung up.

Looking back with the benefit of hindsight, I don't believe that 'phone call was Violla Rubber's idea. It must have been Miss Davis's. So even at that early stage she must have decided that she was going to allow me to be her friend.

One of the formalities that Bette Davis always insisted on from the people she worked with was that they should call her 'Miss Davis'. This was, in my opinion, right and proper. The publicist on *The Anniversary* was not seen after the first day of shooting because he cheerfully called out 'Good morning, Bette.'

Soon afterward I received a 'phone call from her.

'Hello, Roy,' she said.

'Hello, Miss Davis,' I replied politely.

'Hello, Roy,' she repeated, after a significant pause.

'Yes, Miss Davis?'

'It's Bette!' She spat the name out, and then I knew that she had decided I should be a friend rather than just a member of the entourage. It was the beginning of a magic carpet ride for me. It was the beginning of my Auntie Mame story. The extraordinary woman was about to take over my life, throwing open windows onto vistas which I had never dreamed of.

Our friendship grew fast. One visit a week turned into two and then into three. Soon we were together as often as we were apart. It started with visits to the film set, but very quickly turned into evenings at The Chantry, Stanley Kubrick's rambling house in Borehamwood where he edited many of his greatest films, and which Bette had rented for the duration of the shooting.

Violla Rubber was still around for the first few weeks of our friendship, and I was able to see just how badly Bette could treat people if they allowed her to. Bette always liked to buy presents to take back to B.D. after filming abroad, and she dispatched Violla to buy a bathing suit for her well-built, near six-foot tall daughter. When we got back to the house that evening Violla proudly displayed a designer swimsuit which she had purchased at great expense from Fortnum and Mason's. It was the most complicated and bizarre piece of designer engineering. Bette looked at it solemnly for a moment as Violla held it up for inspection.

'Well, put it on, Violla,' she said eventually, 'put it on.'

Violla looked aghast but Bette just stood waiting to see how this poor, plump old woman would force herself into these sparse swathes of material. She was completely merciless, forcing Violla to make an idiot of herself in order to demonstrate how to wear the peculiar garment, until eventually she pulled and struggled a little too hard and ended up in a heap on the floor.

Bette stood triumphantly over her. 'How can I give that to B.D.?' she asked. 'You look ridiculous!'

At the Chantry Violla had found Bette a housekeeper who was her match in every way, and who we re-employed when Bette next came to England. Her name was Mrs Bottoms but Bette called her 'Mrs B'. Mrs B had come up through the ranks of British domestic service and we suspected she had worked in royal households. She was both proud and formal about her position. Bette loved that. She also loved Mrs B's plain English cooking, particularly her boiled potatoes, which reminded me of the worst aspects of British school dinners.

'No potatoes for me tonight, Mrs B,' Bette would protest as Mrs B offered her another steaming bowl. 'They're bad for me . . . oh, all right!' and she would heap them onto her plate with undisguised relish.

Whenever Bette left the house, with the car waiting at the front door to take her away to the studios, Mrs B would always be standing rigidly to attention. She had to say goodbye, and then she would wave to her as she set off down the drive. Her formality meant that Bette never got to know anything more about her personal life. Her room was at the end of a dark corridor and Bette would see a crack of light under the door, and know that she was in and all was well with the house.

One evening we were at the Chantry expecting to have dinner with some admirer of Bette's, but he didn't turn up. Bette decided to start dinner without him. Placing a stately 'Roman' bust on the absent friend's chair, she proceeded to converse with it throughout the meal. She was very funny and made a joke out of the fact that she had been 'stood up' by her admirer.

Whenever Bette took over someone else's house she always changed all the furniture around, to make it more like her own home. However, she was meticulous about taking notes of how things were before she arrived, so that she could put them back exactly the same way when she left. She was also extremely careful with the inventory of the house, which she personally supervised. Quite often she would change her mind several times about how the furniture looked best, and whoever had been dragooned in to do the moving around would be shifting things back and forth as she changed her mind.

Not only did Bette befriend me, she also befriended my mother. The two of them became close almost immediately. While my mother was a great admirer of Bette and her work, she was not in awe of her, and Bette appreciated that. She also appreciated having someone with whom she could gossip about Dorothy Hyman. Dorothy had been my mother's friend many years before but there had been some falling out in the past and my mother and father had always been fonder of the late Neville Hyman than his wife. Now their son Jeremy was married to Bette's beloved daughter, and Bette hated both the son and his mother with almost equal venom. Often I would catch her and my mother giggling about something, and I knew who the object of their jokes was. Bette always referred to Dorothy as 'mother-in-law'. I often thought that her tirades against the Hymans were unfair. My mother, however, who knew more about Dorothy's past, mysteriously suggested that Bette's judgement might be fairer than even she knew. She said Dorothy could be a very 'irritating' woman.

My mother also had to get used to Bette's unpredictable manners while she was working. I knew that before she filmed each scene she needed some quiet moments. My mother was sitting with her in the caravan between takes, chatting happily, when the next moment Bette silenced her with a sharp 'Shut up!' I had to explain that this was actually a compliment. Bette was happy to have us around while she was working, an honour she bestowed sparingly, but she had to have quiet to concentrate when necessary. If it had been someone she cared about less she would have asked them politely to leave; as it was she had simply slipped into character.

One of the first days that I spent on the set, it looked as if filming would have to stop and Bette would have to go home because of the catarrh blocking her nose. The actress Hermione Baddeley had introduced me to a product called Otrivine, which I had been using myself. I dashed out to a local chemist to find a bottle for Bette and after one squirt she was able to work again. Being the pillar of the film, Bette was heavily insured, which meant that everything to do with medical matters had to be passed by the production authorities. It was amazing that she trusted me to such an extent that she took the medicine I recommended without reference to her doctor.

Whenever Bette was filming, her self-discipline was tremendous. No matter who was at the house for dinner she would rise from the table and go to her bedroom at nine o'clock. She got straight into bed, after preparing herself for the next day's shooting, then perhaps she would watch television, or chat to a favoured friend for a short while. Within a few weeks I found that I was the one she asked to accompany her upstairs, and this was a pattern that continued throughout our friendship. Sometimes we would lie on the bed watching movies, sometimes I would be in one of the chairs talking and listening while she bathed in the adjoining bathroom and prepared for bed. It was during these evenings that we found out the most about one another, and she gave me a glimpse into her private life.

There has always been a snobbery amongst people about how to pronounce 'Bette'. Those who think they know pronounce it 'Betty', looking down on those who pronounce it 'Bet' as rather common. One evening we were both watching a televised dramatisation of *Cousine Bette* by Balzac, with Margaret Tyzak in the lead role.

'You know, I'm really "Bet",' she suddenly exclaimed. She went on to explain that when she had chosen her stage-name a friend of her mother's had suggested that she name herself after this Balzac character. So the people who left off the final syllable were correct, but Bette decided it was a little late to change now!

It is hard for me to describe to anyone who does not already know, just how great Bette Davis is. In my eyes she was, and still is, the greatest of film stars. During our friendship I was to find out just how many other people shared this opinion. Bette Davis could attract crowds of fans larger than any pop singer. Everyone wants to meet her and see her. Amongst her Hollywood peers she was able to induce extraordinary, spontaneous mass ovations, even amongst those who had reason to dislike her as a person. She was a queen, a colossus on the world stage. Yet when she and I were together we were just two friends chatting about our lives and the lives of the people around us. It seemed surprising to me that someone so busy could have so much time to spend with me. Because she had always eschewed Hollywood high society, ignoring the spurious glamour of the film industry in favour of dedicated work, she had led a limited social life with a well-chosen circle of friends. The few good friends she did have were back in America. It meant that she had time to befriend someone in England who shared her enthusiasms and was happy to fit in with her unglamorous lifestyle. I was more than happy to spend as much time with her as she would allow, fascinated by the glimpses which she gave me into her career and life.

The Anniversary was not a happy film to work on. The original director was Alvin Rakoff, a highly respected man with a reputation for being slightly tyrannical. On the first day of filming Bette turned up on time. Rakoff was busy with two of the younger players and took no notice of her, leaving her standing on her mark. It might have been his way of trying to bring down the great lady. She stood there for half an hour, spun on her heel and went home to 'phone the producer Jimmy Sangster and complain about her treatment by Rakoff.

Meetings took place to discuss who should replace him, and Bette suggested Roy Baker. Bette had first met Roy in the United States when he was there to direct Marilyn Monroe in *Don't Bother to Knock*. He was an exceptionally nice man and Bette had travelled with him on the Superchief train between New York and Los Angeles. They had spent three days together, with Roy's wife Joan, and got on very well. He had made some workmanlike pictures and, most importantly, I believe Bette felt she could dominate him if necessary.

Bette only liked two other members of the cast. One was Christian Roberts, who I had been representing as an agent, and the other was James Cossins. She took a particular dislike to Sheila Hancock (I believe the feeling was mutual) and when Sheila asked if she might bring the comedian Frankie Howerd to the set to meet her, Bette said she would rather she didn't. She wanted to decide who would and would not meet her. In his biography of Bette, Charles Higham quotes Sheila Hancock extensively:

I acted in the play when it was on stage, and I was acutely aware that Miss Davis wanted to replace me with Jill Bennett for the picture, and was annoyed because Jill wasn't available. I was terrified of what would happen when we started work. I was a working-class actor from the Royal Court Theatre and had no interest in the so-called star system. I wasn't used to venerating a star. I wasn't prepared for Miss Davis's great entourage and for the fawning attitude it had towards her. I was shocked when the producer, Mr Sangster, gave us a lecture saying that Miss Davis liked to be treated with great adulation.

It was very unusual for Bette to be accompanied by more than one or two people, one of whom would be Violla. Knowing Jimmy Sangster very well, I am sure that he did not intend what he said to sound like a lecture. However, it is most certainly correct to welcome a star of Bette's magnitude on the first day of filming.

Miss Hancock continued:

In the very first scene, Miss Davis came down a staircase. It was quite uncalled for by the scene. Everybody in the studio, technicians, the lot, were present, all those not working on *The Anniversary* as well as those who were. And, as she made her descent, everyone clapped on cue. And she went back and did the scene again for the cameras. I was dumbfounded. I thought, 'This is rather silly.' It took me a while to realise this was the way Bette Davis was used to operating. She was a queen after all.

Miss Davis often received applause from film crews with her virtuosity. Sheila Hancock concludes:

She often had rows off set, I heard a lot of shouting from the dressing room next door. People kept getting sacked. There was an awful atmosphere. I heard her say once, very loudly, from next door: 'I hate a good atmosphere on a picture. Every picture I've done where everybody had been hail-fellow-well-met had been a total disaster, and any film that had been miserable to make was a success.' *The Anniversary* proved her wrong.

After watching Bette do a take, Miss Hancock said afterwards, with typical British reticence, 'That was pretty good.'

Bette puffed at a cigarette and glowered. 'Pretty good?' she snapped. 'At least, thank God, somebody has said something. The highest compliment I've had on this picture is "Cut! Print it!" '

The part which Christian Roberts played had originally belonged to Michael Crawford on the stage. When the film was cast however, Crawford wanted Mona Washbourne to play the lead role as she had done in the play when it had been produced in London's West End. When he heard Bette Davis had been cast he refused to play his lead part in the film. He didn't seem to realise that Mona Washbourne was not a name to head the cast of a motion picture. His decision, however, worked to my and Christian's advantage and we were delighted about it.

The result of all this ill-feeling was that the atmosphere on the set became very hard to bear at times, since several members of the original stage cast were also in the film. This was not helped by Bette's paranoia about people whispering. She couldn't bear it if anyone whispered, believing that they were conspiring against her behind her back. In fact most of them were whispering out of respect for her, not wanting to disturb her while she was working, but if she caught them she would lose her temper and demand they stop immediately.

When people find out that you know Bette Davis, and they always do, they all want to know more about her and, if possible, they want to meet her. I soon discovered that Bette was as good as her word. At our first lunch together she had said that she wanted to meet anyone who wanted to meet her, in order to make up her own mind about them. She proved, throughout our relationship, to be totally approachable. If I met someone who I thought was a deserving case I would tell her about them and she would say, 'Then we'll make a day and you can bring them over.' I was careful not to abuse this privilege.

Her fans span every class and every generation. One of my friends at the time was Sir Joseph Lockwood, then Chairman of EMI. With one of the most important jobs in the entertainment industry, Sir Joseph cut a very grand figure. But when he discovered that I knew Bette he was just another admirer.

'Oh Roy, I would love to meet her,' he told me. 'I've got some important people coming from Australia and will be at my country house at the weekend. It would be wonderful if Miss Davis could call in.'

'Okay,' I offered, 'I'll ask her. We are going to be driving in your direction at the weekend. Shall we drop in for tea?'

As I expected, Bette raised no objection to visiting friends of mine and so we drove over in my mini car to Sir Joseph's extraordinary, eccentric, purpose-built home in Berkshire. Sir Joseph had assembled a group of people for the tea party, and greeted Bette like a long-lost friend. He had her sign his EMI visitors book, which contained all the greatest names in music and entertainment for much of the last century, and in which she covered half a page with a massive autograph. He then insisted on showing her round the exotic mansion.

As we started on our tour, surrounded by attentive guests, I noticed Bette shooting me a mischievous glance out of the corner of her eye. By now I recognised this expression. It meant that she had thought of something naughty to do, and my heart sank. In the lounge was a very modern carpet. The design included some enormous nobbles, made up in six-inch-wide knots of wool. It was a strange-looking object. As Bette approached it, chatting away to her host, I saw her place her heel next to one of the nobbles and tumble to the floor. I did not move to her assistance, knowing that she was perfectly capable of making a stage fall without hurting herself. The assembled company, however, were mortified and crowded round the stricken legend, apologising and lifting her back onto her feet. I dare say Sir Joseph could envisage an expensive lawsuit if Bette was injured and had to delay the shooting of her picture.

Later, when we were in the mini heading back to Maidenhead, Bette roared with laughter. 'What a house!' she exclaimed. 'And that carpet! I could have broken my neck!' I didn't say a word; I just looked at her knowingly and then we both burst out laughing. We went back to that strange house on another occasion, and I carefully steered Bette round the carpet. Many people, including her daughter, have accused Bette Davis of having no sense of humour, and although she laughed a lot I think that accusation is true. She certainly did not have a sense of humour about herself. But I will always remember the laughing we did in those years. Bette was young in her attitudes, lovely and naughty.

During this early period in our relationship we also went out a lot, especially to restaurants, bumbling around the countryside in my mini. I was the only person she allowed to drive her who wasn't a Rolls Royce trained chauffeur. At one official function which I attended with her, she did have a chauffeur-driven limousine placed at her disposal. During the evening, however, she spotted the chauffeur taking a drink and refused to be driven by him. When we left she climbed into the mini with me, and we had to drive home with the limousine crawling along behind.

During a meal in a restaurant at Princes Risborough, I spotted Patricia Neal and her husband Roald Dahl across the dining room. I told Bette they were there and she could hardly believe it. She and Pat had been together at Warners, and there was a great actresses' re-union in the middle of the restaurant. Over the following months we visited the Dahls and they came to us several times and we became very friendly.

The distinguished New York lawyer, Arnold Weissberger, who was a friend of mine, told me that he was compiling a book of photographs he had taken of famous stars. He was gathering the pictures with the help of his good friend Milton Goldman, the world's most celebrated actor's agent. Between them they had managed to collect pictures of just about everyone, but Bette still eluded them. Because I liked Arnold so much, I said I would organise it for him. He and Milton were due to visit the Dahls for tea one weekend, and Bette and I were there for lunch. I told Pat what I was doing and then set about keeping Bette at the house until the others arrived. Unfortunately Arnold and Milton were delayed and Bette became very impatient and puzzled at my behaviour. In the end I had to give in and we went out to the car just as Arnold and Milton drew up. She wasn't too keen on the idea of the picture but agreed, and Arnold took an interesting portrait of her with Patricia Neal. I was very pleased to be able to do a favour for such a good friend, and also pleased that Bette would be in his book.

One evening she expressed a wish to go to the Thatched Barn restaurant which is attached to a public house outside Borehamwood. When we got there it was very full but I managed to find her a corner table in the bar while we waited for our table in the restaurant. I had told them it was for Bette Davis and asked for a discreet booth. We had had a couple of scotches when a man came up to Bette and asked if she would mind letting him take her photograph. Bette very politely declined since one person doing it would alert the whole pub, but she said that if the man would give me his name and address she would be happy to send him a signed photograph. I stood up to take the information, but the man looked at me, said 'I've lost interest', and walked off. Bette took no notice of the incident, but I felt disturbed.

A little while later we were still sitting and talking, having a very pleasant time, when there was a jostling and a ferocious flash which nearly blinded me. The man had pushed his way between us and let a flash off directly in Bette's face. I was furious and was all for chasing after him, using her expression, 'I'm gonna kill him!' but Bette pulled me back down onto my seat.

'Forget it, Roy,' she said calmly. 'Can you imagine the headlines, "Bette Davis in pub brawl"?'

I managed to control my anger and we went through into the dining room, where we were seated in a secluded booth. To my horror, on the wall above our heads was a large framed picture of Bette and her last husband Gary Merrill. I apologised profusely but she wasn't bothered. It turned out that the reason she had wanted to come to the place was because she and Gary had been before and really liked it. That night I began to realise that when you are Bette Davis you can never really lead a private life.

There was a dinner dance in the restaurant that evening and Bette kept begging me to dance with her. I was very embarrassed because, despite having started my career in the music industry, I have never taken the time to learn how to dance. She was very disappointed and explained to me how much she enjoyed dance music. Her first husband Harmon O. Nelson had been a band-leader at the Hollywood Roosevelt Hotel in the 1930s and she had always loved to go and listen. I was later to discover that she had a magnificent collection of old 78 rpm records from the era.

It wasn't long before I realised that I was way out of my depth financially. I was still young and struggling, and could not afford the costs of entertaining an eminent person continuously. I had to come clean, terrified that it would mean I couldn't see as much of her in the future.

'Bette,' I said, 'I love being with you. I've enjoyed everything we've done together in the last few weeks but I simply can't afford to keep it up. I haven't the resources to eat out so often.'

She nodded matter-of-factly. 'That's okay,' she said, 'don't worry about it.'

From that day on she never, ever allowed me to be embarrassed about money in her company. Towards the end of any meal we might take in a restaurant, I would feel a tap on the knee. She wanted the man to pay the bill, so she would pass me the money out of sight. She always came out prepared with the right amount, and she never, ever referred to the matter again.

At the end of shooting on *The Anniversary*, some friends invited us both down to their house in the country. We were rather late arriving and only my friend and his grandmother were there to greet us, since his mother and step-father had gone out to a drinks party. When they returned, Bette was very impressed with the stepfather, who was a handsome and charming man – and had had a few drinks. They chatted for a while and then our host said, 'And what do you do for a living?'

Without batting an eyelash the great star answered, 'I'm an actress.'

When we came down the next morning Bette caught my arm and pulled me into a corner, whispering conspiratorially.

'You've got to help me find out what's going on,' she said. 'My room was right above theirs and they argued all the time. I spent the whole night with my ass in the air and my ear to the floor.'

We then went in to breakfast, which was laid out very grandly on silver salvers, and soon discovered that our host and hostess argued constantly, about absolutely everything.

One evening at The Chantry, when we had retired to her room, she had climbed into bed and I was sprawled at her feet. She had her Rollerdex beside her, a ring-binder system for storing names, addresses and telephone numbers. She was flicking through the pages and every so often she would rip one out, screw it up and toss it contemptuously into a waste basket. Each page that flew into the basket represented a person whom Bette no longer wanted to be part of her life. It was then that I first wondered how long I would be able to hang on before I too was tossed aside into her waste basket.

4

My First Visit to Twin Bridges

When the filming of *The Anniversary* was over, Bette had to fly back home to America. I was afraid that this might be the end of our relationship. I was, after all, only charged with her 'care' during the filming in England. Once she had returned to her friends and relations at home, why should she need me any more? I was determined that if the friendship lapsed, it would not be through lack of effort on my behalf. Bette assured me that the same was true on her side, and insisted that I visit her in Westport Connecticut as soon as possible. She told me how much better America would be for me than England, how much easier it would be to establish myself in the business, how she would be able to help me and how much fun we would have together. She wanted to show me her new house and for me to stay with her. I promised I would be out at the first opportunity, but what if I turned up there and was, once again, an outsider in her life, watching from the sidelines, just as I had watched her movies all those years before? It was possible that surrounded by her friends and family she would see me in a different light.

She had moved to Westport to be near to B.D. and Jeremy – much to their obvious annoyance. She had found a house which she loved and which she was busily turning into a home, having previously been living in the guest house of an old drama-school friend in the area while she had house-hunted. Soon after her departure, her letters from America started to arrive, and they encouraged me. After each one there was often a gap of a few weeks and I always looked forward to the arrival of the next. Not really knowing what was happening over there, I imagined that if she became involved in another film our regular correspondence would be reduced.

When her letters did arrive they were always warm. She told me how she thought of me whenever she looked at her charm

29

bracelet. (I had given her a golden heart for it.) She wanted to know why I didn't go to live over in America. She remembered the good times we had had in England and kept me informed on everything she did to the house, asking me when I would be out to see it. One letter ended on a sad note: 'Life goes along,' she said, 'in its lonely way – and I mean lonely – the home is great - but that's not life – Love, Bette.'

So it was with a mixture of longing to see her and trepidation at the welcome I would receive from the family, that I set out for New York a few months later. I was staying with a friend in Manhattan and I knew that he was also a great admirer of Bette's. The two of us often used to do Bette Davis impersonations together in the days before I had actually met the lady. I arrived at his apartment on a Tuesday and, before I had even recovered from my jet lag, I couldn't resist making the 'phone call to Westport.

'Mind if I use your 'phone?' I asked casually.

'Of course not.'

'I'm just going to call Bette Davis.'

'Oh yeah, sure!' he laughed.

'I am, honestly!' I pointed to the extension at the other end of the room: 'Listen in if you want.'

'Okay.' He was still grinning, thinking I was playing some practical joke.

Bette always answered the 'phone in the same way, with a simple, sweeping, 'Yeees.' I looked across at my friend. He had stopped laughing and was listening with wide eyes and a dropped jaw.

'It's Roy, Bette,' I said. 'I'm in New York.'

'Come for the weekend.'

'Certainly, when does the weekend start?'

'Tomorrow,' she snapped, and hung up. Just as she always answered the 'phone in the same way, she always hung up without saying goodbye. It left people who didn't know her with the distinct feeling that they had managed to offend her. It was a habit that used to drive us all wild.

This was rather embarrassing, since I was supposed to be staying with my friend for a few days and the next day was only Wednesday. Because it was a command from Bette Davis, however, he was very understanding. So it was that the next day I went to

Grand Central Station and took a train out to Westport, Connecticut for the first of many visits.

Grand Central Station itself is a breathtaking experience, huge and hectic. I felt that I was setting out on a real adventure. It is just over an hour's journey to Westport on the Newhaven Commuter, but the little town is far away from the bustle of Manhattan. I was so desperate to see Bette again that every minute of the journey was an agony. The train seemed to move more slowly than I'd thought was possible. At every stop a wheeltapper would laboriously circle the train tapping each of the wheels to check that it was sound. Finally we arrived at a small station, seemingly in the middle of Connecticut. The sign said 'Westport and Saugatuck'. It looked more suitable for the Mid-West a century before than for the luxurious green belt of New England. I climbed down the steps from the train and found that Bette had sent a car for me.

On future visits I was to take taxis. The first time this happened there was a cab waiting at the station when I arrived and I climbed in. To my amazement two other people jumped in as well. In Westport, taxi sharing was standard practice. I didn't need to give the taxi driver an address, I simply said 'Bette Davis's house', and he knew where to go. Locally, she was the most important person in town, and that was in an area where her neighbours included Paul Newman and Joanne Woodward, and many of the richest people in America.

It is a delightful hick town, full of beautiful houses in their own grounds. Bette's house did actually have an address: it was called Twin Bridges, Number One Crooked Mile. The house name referred to the two bridges which led onto her property from the road, crossing the small tributary to the River Saugatuck.

As I already knew, wherever Bette travelled in the world, she always arranged her homes to look the same. Much of the furniture actually followed her back and forth between the East and West coasts of America. Her favourite pieces were the Diana table, with its swivelling centre piece, a set of dining room chairs which were actually commodes, and a large chaise-longue. The wall on the right-hand side of the staircase as you went upstairs was covered in pictures of the great and famous: Somerset Maugham, John F. Kennedy, Lyndon B. Johnson and Carl Sandburg. Joan Crawford was in the spare room. On the other side of the stairs were Bette's

Oscar nominations, all ten of them. It was a beautiful, homely house, into which Bette welcomed me with open arms. I was to become very comfortable there over the following years.

On that first arrival the warmth of her welcome was wonderful. She came running out of the house to embrace me. When she finally let me go I picked up my cases to carry them indoors. She became suddenly stern.

'No man does chores in my home!' she snapped, and dragged the heavy cases in herself, refusing to listen to my gallant and embarrassed protests.

'This is your room.' She showed me proudly into the spare room which she had decorated very prettily and in which she had placed objects for my special use. I immediately felt at home and knew that any anxieties I might have been harbouring had been unfounded.

The Oscars were on the mantlepiece in the sitting room, together with awards from all over the world. There was also a table with a glass top displaying numerous tributes to her in the form of medals and orders. As well as the sitting room there was a River Room, which overlooked the river from the side of the house. This is where she kept all her books, scripts and memorabilia. There were books everywhere, since the local bookshop delivered most of the new titles every few weeks. I spent an afternoon once browsing through her bookshelves and found a baby book which recorded in loving detail her name and her parents' names, the date and place of her birth and weight at birth. She had copies of her scripts bound in red leather, some of them covered in masses of hand-written notes. I was interested to see that the screenplay which had the fewest notes was *All About Eve*, possibly her greatest part.

Her spacious en-suite bedroom had a queen-sized bed and many photographs of the family. Her private bathroom had a sunken bathtub. There was also a room for her son Michael, a small spare room, and a sun room which doubled as her adopted daughter Margot's room when she was there.

On my many visits I moved from room to room depending on how many of the children or other friends were staying, but much of our time was always spent in the kitchen. There was a maid there the first time I visited, but Bette was never comfortable with servants in my time and much preferred to run her own home – which she did beautifully.

B.D. and Jeremy lived about four miles down the road in a house called Wildwoods, on Steep Hill Road, and B.D. was often dropping in or calling for chats. Sometimes Jeremy would also be there for dinners at one or other of their houses, and usually when that happened there was a definite air of tension.

At Twin Bridges I was to see another side of Bette Davis. She was a perfect hostess. Her cooking was good and imaginative, although sometimes she would use too many spices. She always insisted that you were served second helpings, although the first ones were overly generous. She did not accept being full as an excuse and she would practically force-feed you, until you felt thoroughly ill. While she was cooking breakfast she was thinking about what to do for lunch, and during lunchtime preparations she was planning for dinner. At times she would cheat and pass off a shop-bought cake or dish as home-made – nobody dared to contradict her. She liked silver, which she kept highly polished all the time. There were heavy sets of cutlery with her initials engraved on them, and the stands and containers for everything from sauce to toast gleamed and sparkled.

One evening we were watching television together in her room and a comedienne came on, doing an impersonation of Bette. She hated impersonations, never seeing anything about herself to laugh at. I always told her that she should look on them as the sincerest form of flattery. That evening it was the second or third time there had been some reference to her on the screen, but she didn't seem to have noticed.

'Bette,' I said, 'you are *so* famous. You are more famous than any of them. Just look at how many people refer to you, even in this one evening. Everyone in the world knows who you are.'

She shrugged. 'What do you want for breakfast tomorrow?' she asked. Bette knew I liked breakfast and always got up herself to prepare it for me, although she was not a great breakfast eater herself when she was not working.

When she gave dinner parties, which wasn't often, she would do all the cooking and waiting herself. If there were more than three or four of us, she would not sit at the table with her guests, but would set herself up a card table by the kitchen door and eat there, in between dashing around to serve people. It tended to make guests who did not know her well very nervous. While they were attempting to make polite conversation at the table, they

33

would be aware of this enormous presence sitting outside the circle, listening, and occasionally silencing everyone else with a loud interjection. When she spoke, of course, everyone had to turn to listen, which completely disrupted the flow of conversation. Nothing, however, could persuade her to change this habit, even at Christmas. She simply couldn't see the point of sitting down at the table with everyone else if she was going to be constantly popping in and out of the kitchen.

As I had quickly discovered with the suitcases, she disliked anyone else doing anything in her house, particularly men. She wouldn't even allow me to help her with wood for the fire. At four o'clock each winter's day, as dusk began to fall, she would go round every room, turning on the lights to make the house glow warmly in the evening and turning down everyone's beds. She liked to have a roaring log fire in the sitting room. She also liked to keep the house a little warmer than I found comfortable. She liked it at around 70 degrees and I preferred it at around 60. Every time she left the room I would quickly turn the thermostat down, and each time she passed it she would turn it back up with a puzzled expression.

When she was at home she dressed very casually, usually in slacks and outsized men's shirts. She had actually been wearing the 'Annie Hall' look for decades before Diane Keaton made it famous and won an Oscar for the film. She had a collection of funny hats which she liked to wear. Her favourite was one of the Castro-style caps. Because a film actress spends so much of her working life being primped and pampered, Bette couldn't be bothered to do her hair or make herself up if she was just going to be around the house. It was much easier to pull on a scarf, or one of the hats which hung on the hat stand by the front door.

Her smoking habits have always been one of her trademarks, and she knows how to use cigarettes as props to the utmost effect. She seldom smokes more than a couple of puffs of each one before she puts it down or stubs it out. She often forgot she already had one going, and there might be two or three burning away in ashtrays at the same time. It was a constant juggling act and I did sometimes find cigarette burns on her bedclothes which worried me greatly. She didn't inhale them and consequently, although she got through a lot of packs, she didn't do as much actual smoking as it seemed. She also liked to use the sort of matches which will strike against anything rough. If she was sitting opposite you she might well lift up your foot and strike one on the sole of your shoe, or under a nearby table. It was a clever, extravagant, dramatic gesture. She always kept a supply of both cigarettes and matches near her and all over the downstairs rooms in silver or china containers. She would light them with a dramatic puff, almost seeming to snap at the cloud of smoke as it drifted back out of her mouth.

As well as enjoying the role of housewife, she liked playing nurse. Once, when I showed a slight sign of having a cold, she forced me into bed and insisted that I drank a honey and lemon concoction, even though it was hot enough to take the roof off my mouth. She would have been great as one of those old-fashioned matrons who ruled hospitals with a rod of iron.

All through her life she had been torn between her desire to have the greatest career possible and her longing to be a simple, home-loving woman at the centre of a happy family. When she was married to Arthur Farnsworth, her second husband, she bought a farm called Butternut at Sugar Hill in New Hampshire. She often talked about it. She loved feeling she was part of the local village life, and she loved the simple pleasures of being warm and snug inside the cosy house while the snow and wind swirled about outside. She would work in the barns, tossing the hay, and would press and lay out her own linen, airing beds, plumping pillows and shaking out blankets. She would work in the garden, cook and make jam just like any other New England housewife.

In her book *My Mother's Keeper*, Bette's daughter B.D. remembers many happy times there as a small child. By that time the original house was occupied by a caretaker and his family, but Bette had built two other houses on the estate. One was a white, Colonial-style building in the woods, surrounded by stone terraces and English-style formal gardens. Bette's mother Ruthie moved in there and Bette built another house from a barn which she had moved, timber by timber, silo included, to the top of the hill, and converted into a lodge. Everything about it was on a grand scale, retaining the original features of the barn.

When she married William Grant Sherry, the family's main home moved to Laguna, the well-known resort town on the coast south of Los Angeles, where Sherry came from and where Bette's

35

cousins the Favors lived. The new house was modest in size, but enjoyed spectacular ocean views from its cliff-top vantage point.

When married to Gary Merrill, she moved to a large house standing alone on a peninsula overlooking the ocean at Cape Elizabeth in Maine. One of her chief delights, she used to tell me, was eating the local lobsters, which they cooked in pitsbeaches near her home. The house was called Witch Way. B.D. remembered a long dirt road approaching the house which passed through an apple orchard and a pond before arriving at a circular driveway. She remembered farm animals, flower beds, lily banks and rock gardens, vegetables and a greenhouse, all tended by Bette. She attacked the job of home-making with all the vigour which she put into her professional projects.

It all seemed a long way from the mad, bad, sad and tormented women she had been famous for playing on the screen. But underneath the surface of this seemingly cosy, warm, loving family life, bad blood was flowing like volcanic lava, and before long I was to see it burst to the surface in dazzling, scalding eruptions, sweeping both the innocent and the guilty before it indiscriminately.

5

Bette and B.D.

I was very nervous about how Bette's existing friends and relatives would take to me. I was, after all, a complete interloper into their lives and they had no idea who I was or where I had come from. I think to start with they thought I was just a fan who had somehow managed to get himself into Miss Davis' good graces. When they discovered that I was involved in the business in a variety of ways, they began to relax more and eventually they grew to be my friends. B.D. was particularly sweet to me, and inscribed a book she gave me one Christmas with a note saying how pleased they were to have me as a close friend of the family. I appreciated that gesture very much.

By this time Bette had called an uneasy truce with Jeremy Hyman. She realised that the marriage was obviously not going to break up and that if she wanted to be near to her daughter, she had to be polite to him. There was no mistaking the dislike which Bette and Jeremy had for each other. Although I could see that she deliberately baited him, I had to agree that he was often unnecessarily difficult. She was, after all, his mother-in-law, and I think that he should have made more concessions. Equally there were many occasions when a little self-control from Bette would have avoided some very unpleasant scenes. She, however, disliked him too deeply to be able to let bygones be bygones. Many times, when we were alone at the house, she would tell me just what it was that had hurt her most.

Firstly there had been the matter of the wedding. Bette hadn't approved of the match in the first place but when she realised that B.D.'s mind was made up she had reluctantly accepted the situation. She then insisted on giving them a big wedding. She went to a lot of trouble to organise a perfect day for them both, and couldn't help feeling a glow of pride when she saw her daughter resplendent in her wedding dress. Her exact words were, 'B.D.

sailed up the aisle like a battleship,' which I am convinced she
meant to be a compliment, and which was also probably a very
accurate description. It wasn't until later that she discovered that
the whole day had been a sham put on for her benefit. The couple
had actually got married a few days before for tax reasons, but
had decided to let Bette believe that she was overseeing a genuine
wedding. This version was told to me by Peggy Shannon. Bette
and she may have embellished it a little in order to improve her role
as the aggrieved party. In her book B.D. remembers it differently,
claiming that her mother knew about the civil wedding all along,
although she didn't like the idea. If this was so, it was typical of
the ways in which Bette would dramatise stories to put across her
own viewpoint, which in the case of B.D. and Jeremy was that
they treated her shamefully at every turn or rather that Jeremy
had treated her badly. She never, ever blamed B.D. to me and
seemed convinced that B.D. was acting on Jeremy's wishes.

'Why didn't they tell me?' she would ask, again and again. 'It
was only $3,000. I would have given him the damn money for the
taxes if it meant I could see my daughter married.'

It then took the young couple seven years to conceive a child.
Bette was desperately impatient to be a grandmother, and when
B.D. finally became pregnant she was overjoyed. She rang me in
England to tell me and could hardly contain her excitement. She
was convinced that the baby would be a girl. However, when B.D.
was admitted to hospital in labour, Jeremy did not tell Bette until
it was all over. Bette was at home when she learned she had a
grandson, Ashley, while she would dearly have loved to have been
with B.D. at the hospital. Jeremy and B.D. feared that if she
turned up at the hospital it would attract the press and she would
upset everyone from the doctors and nurses to B.D. herself. Bette
was absolutely distraught at missing the event she had been looking
forward to for so long, and while it was understandable that Jeremy
would prefer it if she wasn't there to make his life difficult with
unnecessary dramatising, it was still unkind of them to shut her
out.

As an outsider it was easy for me to see how unnecessary most
of the family hurt was. If they had been just a little more tolerant
and considerate of one another's feelings, all the later unpleasantness could have been avoided and Bette would have been able to

keep her family around her and would not now be the sad, lonely figure that I'm told she is.

One Christmas Eve we went over to B.D.'s house for dinner. I had been told by Jeremy of a Christmas surprise he was planning for Bette. Soon after we arrived Jeremy and another friend mysteriously disappeared out into the dark, snowy night. They returned an hour or two later, refusing to say where they had been. Dinner continued fairly peacefully and as Bette and I returned home the car lights swept across the snow-covered lawn in front of Twin Bridges, illuminating a large, wrapped parcel.

'Oh, the darlings!' she exclaimed. 'I know what they've done – they've given me a bird bath, just what I've always wanted. How wonderful! I must look at it.'

'Wait till Christmas morning,' I pleaded. 'Jeremy has gone to so much trouble to make it a surprise for you, please wait until the morning – they wanted you to draw open your curtains and see the birdbath on the lawn in front of your bedroom.'

'I can't wait,' she announced, and ran across the lawn to tear away the paper. It was indeed a stone bird bath. It must have nearly killed them to carry it across the lawn. 'It's wonderful!' She was beside herself with joy. 'I must ring them and thank them now!'

Again I tried to stop her. 'Please Bette, wait until the morning, and at least try to pretend you were surprised by it!'

'No, I shall ring them now.'

She did ring them. It was no big deal because she loved the present and appreciated the trouble they had been to. But if she had just stopped and considered their feelings for a little longer, she could have made their Christmas surprise perfect.

Often I thought that Jeremy exercised admirable self-control when she baited him, but every so often he must have decided that enough was enough. On a later visit to Westport I arrived at Twin Bridges in the usual taxi, but the Great Lady did not emerge to greet me and pick up my cases as she normally did. The taxi driver moved as slowly as he possibly could but had to leave disappointed at not seeing her. As I made my way into the house I could hear sobbing in the kitchen, and I found Bette with her head in her arms.

'What on earth is the matter?'

'B.D. 'phoned,' she sniffed. 'She and Jeremy are throwing a welcome home party for you tonight, but I'm not invited.'

'Oh, don't be ridiculous. I'm your guest, I'm not going anywhere without you.' I immediately picked up the 'phone and called B.D. 'Hi, B.D., it's Roy. I hear you're throwing a party for me tonight. That's very sweet of you. . . .' We exchanged a few pleasantries. 'So what time shall your mother and I arrive?' I asked.

After a few moments' silence B.D. replied, 'Seven o'clock.'

'What did she say?' Bette asked as I hung up.

'She said seven o'clock.'

'But what did she say about me?'

'She didn't say anything about you.'

I believe that if Bette had not ended our friendship so abruptly and cruelly, I could have helped her to retain her links with B.D. It required someone with a certain knowledge of the family troubles to re-build the bridges as quickly as they destroyed them, and at least I could act from Bette's end of the receiver.

Despite the fact that she would never allow a man to do anything in her houses, Bette was convinced that Jeremy treated her daughter like a slave, which was obviously untrue. One afternoon when we were at their house, Jeremy said to B.D., 'Why don't you make some of your milkshakes, darling, the ones Roy likes?'

'Why should she?' challenged Bette. It was sometimes hard to see why she deliberately wanted to stir up unpleasantness and dissention on days when we should all have been perfectly happy.

In all the years I knew them, I could never quite work out how B.D. and Jeremy managed to live. They always seemed to have some new scheme for making money, such as setting up an agency for solving problems like recruiting domestic servants, but the ideas never came to anything. They lived very comfortably indeed, but I don't know how much Bette contributed to their family pot. In her book *This 'n That*, Bette claims that she has been B.D.'s 'Keeper' for many years, and she did help them out with money when their businesses ran into trouble. At another stage Jeremy got into the music business and Bette asked me, as a favour to her, to take a consignment of albums back to Britain for him and deliver them to various people. I did it for Bette rather than for Jeremy, who I really did not like.

Jeremy's mother, Dorothy, was another irritant to Bette. Doro-thy's sister, Mrs Elliott Hyman, also lived in Westport, so Dorothy used to pay quite frequent visits and always ended up annoying Bette.

Michael, Bette's adopted son, was away at college for much of the time when I first knew her. When I did meet him he was always extremely pleasant, and he went on to become a successful lawyer with a life well away from his adoptive mother's reach. He was a handsome, blonde boy, who in the end was to supplant B.D. in his mother's affections but, at this time, was very much in second place. Despite this he always seemed to get a smoother ride than his sister, although there was one dinner where he had the 'affrontery' to suggest that Richard Nixon was going to be the next president of the USA. He hadn't for a moment suggested that he liked the idea but Bette still turned on him for even suggesting that such a thing was possible. 'I'm a loyal Democrat,' she shouted, 'and if you dare to mention that man's name in my house you'll get out and not come back.' Of course Nixon did become president quite soon afterwards.

Michael, like B.D., was fortunate to meet the partner he was going to marry very early on, which I think Bette found rather boring, as she had been hoping for a string of exciting affairs and potential daughters-in-law to terrorise. Michael and his girlfriend Chou, who lived down the road on Crooked Mile, needed to spend some time alone together so one evening Bette and I left them together downstairs and went up to her bedroom to watch television. I remember they were showing *Alexander's Ragtime Band*, and we were lying on our stomachs on the bed singing along with Ethel Merman. In fact Bette was doing most of the singing, loudly but not very tunefully. She prided herself on knowing all the songs as her first husband, Harmon Nelson, and his band had played them at the Hollywood Roosevelt Hotel, but I'm not sure that she got all the lyrics quite right.

After a while Bette suggested that we should sneak to the top of the stairs and spy on the young couple. She was like a naughty schoolgirl, peeping through the banisters. Michael and Chou seemed to be right in the middle of love-making, which delighted Bette, and after a quick peek we returned to Ethel Merman.

When Michael and Chou got married, Chou's mother organised everything. She catered caviar and champagne for honoured guests, while the rest were offered something different and much less expensive. Bette told Michael to invite some of his college friends and a dozen of them showed up for his stag party and then for the wedding. At the end of the ceremony Bette gathered this group up with, 'Come on boys, come with old Mother Merrill,' and got them all into one car. She rushed them to the reception before the bride and groom even had time to leave the church, and she pointed them at the caviar and champagne, which they duly demolished before anyone else had arrived.

When Bette's marriage to Gary Merrill broke up there was a long and bitter fight over access to Michael, with Bette claiming that Gary was an unfit influence on the child and trying to keep them apart. She wasn't able to succeed, but so much bitterness must have been hard for a young boy to cope with. Despite this unpromising start to his life, Michael has succeeded in becoming a successful and well-balanced man. His marriage has remained sound, he is a practising attorney and has provided Bette with grandchildren which she sees just enough to keep everyone sane.

Finally there was Margot, a beautiful teenage girl with the mind of a five-year-old. Bette had adopted both Michael and Margot while she was married to her last husband, Gary Merrill. Much of Margot's time was spent in an institution in up-state New York but when she did come home Bette did her best to make her a normal part of the family. At times, however, the bully in Bette would surface, even against this poor, simple girl.

You could talk to Margot about a lot of things, and people didn't always realise she was retarded when they started a conversation. She would talk, for instance, about the Beatles, whom she loved. She would speak very shyly and then she would gently start to rock backwards and forwards very slowly, which meant she was getting tired. She had tremendous sexual urges and she was very beautiful. Any boy that saw her was attracted. She could be very useful about the house, but she needed constant supervision.

At breakfast one day Margot came down with her long, dark hair in a mess. Bette was in a foul mood, and ordered her to go and fetch her hairbrush. As the girl left the room I ventured to say, 'Poor Margot.'

'No,' Bette snarled, 'not poor Margot. Poor me! She doesn't know, I do!'

When Margot came back with the brush, Bette began pulling it through her hair with such violence that I thought she was going to break her neck. Margot sat passively, saying nothing. I tried to interject, telling Bette that the hair looked fine now, but she wouldn't stop. For a few minutes I truly feared for Margot's life. I was also aware that the girl was immensely strong, as many retarded people are, and had she turned on her mother there would have been little I could have done to rescue her.

One morning Margot was in bed with Bette and Bette was bossing her around. Margot suddenly turned on her.

'You're not my mother,' she shouted, 'you can't say this to me.'

'Of course I'm your mother,' Bette shouted back. 'What do you think I've been doing all these years? Where would you be without me? Who do you think paid for you? Who do you think bought all your clothes?' Then she hit her, which I thought was taking a great chance, since Margot was much bigger and much stronger than Bette.

One evening when I was standing in front of the sitting-room fire, Margot came over to talk to me.

'Wouldn't it be funny,' she said, 'if I threw Mother onto the fire.' I moved aside very fast indeed. Not only could she have thrown Mother, she could have thrown me as well.

Having had four husbands added a few more tensions to the family atmosphere, and you could never tell when the past would rise to the surface. Bette appeared, very successfully, on Dinah Shore's television Tribute to her, and I went along with her. At the end of the show members of the audience can actually come forward and talk to the stars if they are keen enough. That night I was waiting while Bette finished talking to Dinah and Jane Fonda, and a young man came up to me. He introduced himself as Harmon Nelson's son. The boy really wanted to meet the great film star to whom his father had been married. I told him to wait where he was and I would go and prepare Bette for him. I took her behind the scenery and told her what had happened. Her first reaction was horror.

'Dammit! Get me out of here, Roy,' she panicked. 'I don't want to talk to him.'

I managed to calm her down and persuade her that it would mean a lot to the boy to be able to talk to her. Finally she agreed and was very polite to him, asking after his father, who had been very ill, and exchanging pleasantries. She didn't seem moved by the experience. It made me realise just how many events and people there had been in her life before I had even met her, and how complicated all the relationships must be inside her mind.

Right from the time when she was a small girl, Bette took her family relationships very seriously. For many years the most important person in her life was her mother. She always said that she owed everything to 'Ruthie' and she never begrudged her anything once she could afford it. She also felt fiercely responsible for her younger sister Barbara, who was always known as Bobby.

From the day Bette was born Ruthie was determined that she would be a star, and lavished all her love and energy onto her first-born. Bette used to say that the moment she popped her head out, Ruthie 'knew' that she was destined for something. Poor Bobby was to remain in her sister's shadow all her life. From childhood Bobby showed signs of mental disturbance, which were to make her dependent on Bette. She was subject to severe nervous attacks bordering on schizophrenia, which finally led to a complete collapse. What made it worse was that Bobby too would have liked to have been an actress but she did not show any talent. At one stage she had to go into a home and was put into isolation, hysterically screaming that Bette had taken away her chances of a career. As Bette became more famous, Bobby became almost her servant during her periods at home, with Bette paying all medical bills.

Bette had purchased a family plot at Forest Lawn cemetery in Burbank. The famous cemetery actually overlooks Warner Brothers Studios and Bette enjoyed the idea that she would be haunting them from the grave. She never forgot the day that she finished at the studio.

'Do you know, Roy,' she told me, 'I did my last shot, went back to my dressing room, packed up my bags to leave after eighteen years and no-one came to say goodbye? I just went through the gates on my own.' The story is a pointed illustration of her unpopularity amongst fellow workers.

The plot contains a restricted number of places, and Bette knew exactly who she wanted to be in there with her. Her mother Ruthie and sister Bobby came first. She also wanted B.D. and Michael (but not their partners) to join her and Bobby's daughter Fay.

'When I go I don't want B.D. to fly West,' she said. 'I don't want a funeral, I just want to be taken to the plot at five in the morning and laid to rest, without anyone knowing.'

44

When she was dwelling on her own mortality, she would also muse about the fleetingness of fame.

'When I go,' she would say, 'I doubt if I will warrant more than a mention on the bottom right-hand corner of the front pages, if that.' I think she underestimated her popularity, but we will see.

Despite all the ups and downs of her relationship with B.D., and despite the fact that the two women now seem to be separated by too wide a gulf ever to be bridged, I believe that for Bette blood will always be the most important tie. When the time comes for Bette's will to be read, I feel sure that B.D. and her children will still be major beneficiaries together, of course, with Michael and his family.

6

Friends and Neighbours

Two other characters who were to play parts in Bette's life at that time were Vik Greenfield and Peggy Shannon. Peggy was one of the top Hollywood hairdressers, and had performed the miraculous task of befriending both Joan Crawford and Bette Davis. In the end she was one of the most faithful friends Bette ever had. She too was a grandmother, and she spent time with Bette and me on the East and West coasts of America, and in London. She had met Bette on *Baby Jane*, where she was working for Joan Crawford. She told me the story.

'One day on *Baby Jane*, Joan called me and said, "Peg, we're just doing a rehearsal, but come on in and keep me company." I just adored Joan and so I said okay, I took the dogs for a walk for her, had lunch with her and that sort of thing.

'That day the director Bob Aldrich introduced me to Miss Davis and then took me aside. "Now Peggy," he said, "we're going to start shooting tomorrow. Miss Davis's hairdresser isn't here but she has ordered a wig. Would you pick it up and bring it back to show to her?" '

Peggy was happy to oblige, and took the wig to Bette, who couldn't believe her eyes.

'It looked like a Shirley Temple wig,' Peggy explained, 'all little curls. So anyway, Miss Davis took it to Mr Aldrich and said, "We can't work. I won't wear it. I just won't wear it." She made me so nervous.'

Bob Aldrich asked Peggy to see what she could do, as he definitely wanted to start shooting the next day. Peggy scurried off to MGM, which had been her home studio and where she was well known, and dived into the hairdressing and make-up department. She rummaged around in the bottom drawer where the wigs were kept. She knew all the wigs were there that had been worn by the stars in the days gone by. She found one that had been worn by Joan Crawford in 1926.

'I didn't say anything,' she said, 'I just took the wig back to Miss Davis. It looked all dried out, overbleached and everything. She was with the designer trying on this bright dress with all the ruffles. She tried on the wig and yelled, "It's the nuts!" I thought she said I was nuts, and I just sat there, stunned, as she did all these turns in the wig. Then she said that this was the first time she had been able to feel the part of Baby Jane. She told me that when she was working on the character she thought of her sister Bobby, scuffing her feet on the floor.

'To this day I don't know how we kept that wig together. It was so old. I told Florence, Bette's hairdresser, to be careful about putting it on and taking it off because it was ready to fall apart and we only had one wig. From then on I went back to working for Joan for the rest of the picture, and Miss Davis was quite happy.'

A few years later Peggy was to come back into Bette's life again when she lost her regular hairdresser. At the time Peggy had been working with Eva Gabor while she was making the television series *Greenacres*. Peggy was sent to the Bel Air Hotel to meet Bette who was flying in from New York.

'She walked in and kicked her shoes off,' Peggy remembered later, 'and I picked up the shoes and put them in the closet.' From then on Peggy became a close companion and friend to Bette. Sometimes, if Peggy was not well, Bette would drive out over the Hollywood Hills to her house in the valley and would look after her. Peggy did not fraternise very much with her neighbours, but became something of a local celebrity when some of them saw Bette Davis sweeping out the back yard for her.

Vik Greenfield was a major part of Bette's life at that time. He was basically Bette's majordomo, although his official title was secretary. The three of us were to become very close. Bette actually used to refer to us as the 'Three Stooges'. She discovered him when he was managing a small hotel in Beverly Hills. Violla Rubber had booked her in there, although it was completely unsuitable, and Bette was quite disturbed by it. The only saving grace had been Vik. He brought a coffee pot up to her room and they started talking. He was the most charming and attractive Englishman. Bette took to him immediately and told him she would arrange a job for him at the new motel in Westport. She was as good as her word and Vik came across to the East Coast, but it wasn't long before she offered him a full-time job at Twin Bridges. After he had been there a while she built a spacious apartment for him above the garage, which was just a few paces away from the house.

Vik was an exceptionally nice man, and worked very hard for Bette, but she still enjoyed exercising her power over him. His sister Stephanie Landsman, whose husband Michael was a successful lawyer, lived in New York and Vik would often visit them on his days off, but Bette resented sharing her people with anyone else.

'When is Vik coming back?' she would ask me.

'In a couple of days,' I would assure her.

'But I want him here now!' she would fume.

'What for?'

'I need him.'

There would then follow a furious telephone call to poor Vik who, presuming his job was on the line, would come rushing back to find that there was no reason at all why he couldn't have stayed away a couple more days.

When Bette wrote to me complaining about loneliness at Twin Bridges, and saying that this 'isn't life', Vik had already moved in. Although Vik was company for her, he could not cure her loneliness. I believe she craved to be the centre of a big, warm, loving family, yet her own volatile personality made such a situation impossible. You cannot be a working film star and a homemaker. There are too many weeks spent in hotels, too much worry about where the next good script is going to come from, too much energy needed for the creation of the characters and too much nervous steam built up while giving a performance.

She also made Vik's life lonely, since she would never allow anyone in her entourage to have a private life. When you were with Bette she had to be the centre of your world. That was easy for me, because I came and went. It was no hardship to devote all my attentions to her when I was with her. For Vik, twenty-four hours a day, seven days a week, it was a far more arduous task. Nor did she order me around as she did Vik. I was a friend, not someone on the payroll, and she was forced to respect that.

Bette did not like Vik to entertain his friends at the house, and she certainly didn't countenance anyone around her having a sex life. She seemed to revel in breaking up other people's relationships, always claiming that she knew better than they did what was good for them. Vik's relationship with Bette was very much like that between a mother and devoted son.

During the autumn the lawns at Twin Bridges, which were surrounded with beautiful trees, would become covered in leaves, and Bette was forever looking out the window and saying 'You haven't cleared the leaves, Vik.' The more he worked at it, the more leaves fell, but he never complained – at least not to Bette.

Despite her bossiness, Bette was genuinely fond of Vik and he managed to stay with her for six years. She had a water-hole dug beside the river to catch the fresh water and in the heat of the summer the two of them would sit in the hole to keep cool, playing like two big kids. One bone of contention between them was Vik's Siamese cat, which Bette disliked, and which had to stay locked in his apartment twenty-four hours a day. Later on, this poor cat was to escape from its cage on a flight from New York to Hollywood. Vik was devastated on being presented with an empty cage when the plane was unloaded. The cat, sad and shivering, turned up in the cargo hold later, and survived the experience. Even Bette was concerned for the poor animal and relieved when Vik returned from the airport with it.

Bette was also extremely fond of Stephanie and Michael Landsman, Vik's sister and brother-in-law. When she was in Manhattan she would often ask to sleep on their sitting room couch rather than going to a lonely suite at the Plaza or Lombardy hotels. It was in ways like this that she showed how much she wanted to be part of a family. It didn't stop her, however, from interfering in their marriage and telling Stephanie that she was married to an imperfect husband. Stephanie just laughed, which was the only way to deal with Bette when she started talking like that.

When Vik started working for Bette he didn't drive, so she decided he should learn. She was always nervous in cars and by that time was an unstable driver. If there was someone on the road in front of her she became annoyed, and if there was someone behind her she became annoyed. If she was sandwiched between two cars she was a complete wreck. She knew her driving days were nearing an end, so Vik dutifully learned to drive. On one occasion, however, while driving down to the local store, he failed to convince the car to stop until it had passed right through the shop window and had nearly reached the counter. Fortunately nobody was hurt, and Vik was able to pick up the shopping and return home in a taxi, quaking at the thought of telling Bette what had taken place. As so often happened when there was a major catastrophe, Bette was totally understanding. It was an accident, so why make a fuss about it?

Violla Rubber was still acting as Bette's manager when I first arrived at Twin Bridges. She saw that I was getting closer to the Great Lady than she was and didn't like it. Bette's agent at the time was David Begelman, and the third member of her team was Harold Schiff, a very powerful New York lawyer who also acted as Bette's business manager. Bette wanted me to work for her as her representative in London but Begelman told Schiff that there was no way he would recognise me as having anything to do with Bette Davis professionally. I told Bette this and she said that we would take no notice and do whatever we wanted. I took her word for this, but I was aware that there was something of a conspiracy building up between the grim American trio.

A few weeks before I was due to join Bette for my first Christmas at Twin Bridges, I received a long letter from Violla in the form of instructions on how to be Bette's friend. There were rules such as 'You shall not introduce Miss Davis to homosexuals', and other even sillier pronouncements. Two weeks later I received another letter from her which told me that from now on I could consider myself sacked from Bette's employment, although I wasn't even employed by her. It was only a couple of days before I was due to fly over to Westport. Assuming that the letter had come with Bette's knowledge, I was bewildered and unable to see what I could have done wrong. My plans for Christmas were all made, so I decided to go ahead as if nothing had happened, having no idea what sort of welcome I would receive when I got to Twin Bridges. To my immense relief her welcome was just as charming as ever. I was in the spare room that year because Gary Merrill's brother and sister-in-law were also there with their three children.

I decided not to bring the subject up to begin with, as the other house guests obviously found it difficult getting used to my relationship with Bette. I remember that her sister-in-law happened to see me sitting in Bette's room talking to her while she was in her bathroom, and expressed her horror. Bette's answer was simple.

'We'll just have to keep the door closed, to keep her nose out!' she snapped.

Eventually everyone else had left and we were on our own in the house. It was late in the evening and we were lying on her bed. I decided to broach the subject.

'Did you know I'd been fired?' I asked.

'Fired?' She looked completely blank. 'What do you mean?'

I told her about the two letters. She listened in silence, stood up and walked from the room. A few minutes later she returned with two tumblers full of Scotch. She handed one to me.

'Here,' she said, 'take this. We are going to be up all night.'

She then proceeded to spend the night making transatlantic 'phone calls to my assistant in London and to everyone else, to find out exactly what had been going on. She went on and on asking questions until my head was spinning. The next day, having had virtually no sleep at all, I had to take the train into New York and stay overnight at the then Park Sheraton on Seventh Avenue. As I arrived in my room the 'phone was ringing. It was Bette.

'Roy,' she said, 'you'd better watch out, Violla is after you with a breadknife. Look over your shoulder every step you take. In fact I think you had better come back here.'

'Whatever are you talking about, Bette?'

'I just fired Violla.'

Needless to say I survived Violla's anger at having caused her to lose her job, and David Begelman also faded from Bette's life. Harold Schiff took over all her business dealings and although I know that he disliked me, he realised that my relationship with Bette could be useful to him and so he remained polite and helpful.

These days many of the stars won't leave home without a massive entourage of minders, hairdressers, lawyers, accountants and hangers-on. Bette wasn't like that. She didn't need an entourage. Wherever she went she was looked after by the airlines, the hotel managements and the film companies she was working for. All she needed was one person to travel with her to take care of the practical arrangements and to be company for her after work. There should have been any number of people who would have been delighted to take on the job but it was not so straightforward. Bette seemed unable to have a friendship that she didn't end up destroying, or an employee that she didn't end up bullying and humiliating. It was a constant worry to B.D., particularly as her mother grew older, that no-one could be found to look after her.

All the neighbours in Westport wanted to entertain Bette Davis in their houses and we were never short of invitations, but Bette very seldom took any of them up because she believed that they didn't really want her for herself, only for her name. The loneliness of stardom was brought home to me on one occasion when we did accept an invitation to a cocktail party. I had long ago learnt that if you escort a celebrity to a party the worst thing you can do is hang onto their arm all through the event. Once you are there you need to split up and circulate separately. I was enjoying the party, and was in the middle of a group of people chatting away happily, when I glanced around the room to see if Bette was all right. Over someone's shoulder I saw her, sitting miserably on a sofa with one silent old man for company. She caught my eye and mouthed the words, 'Get me out of here.'

Bette's problem was that her reputation, coupled with her wonderful face, made her a terrifying prospect for most people. Very few ordinary people had the nerve to actually go up to her and introduce themselves. Her success made her an outcast in a society where she should have been an undisputed queen. Unlike other famous queens, she did have a forbidding look – but she was always delightful when strangers did approach her.

Bette did have a few very close friends in Westport. There was Robin Brown and her husband Albert, 'Brownie' to his friends. She had known Robin since they had been at acting school together. And there was Grace Brynolson, a delightful lady who worked as Cookery Editor for *Time-Life* magazine and was a sufficiently strong character in her own right to be able to cope with Bette.

When she was with the Browns Bette was completely relaxed. One evening, when we were going out as a foursome, we arrived at the Browns' home for a drink before going on. As we walked into the house, Robin noticed that Bette's dress had a crease up the back. Without a second thought Bette peeled it off, got out the iron and ironing board and proceeded to stand there in her petticoat, pressing it.

Even with these close friends, however, she would sometimes shy away from social contact. One New Year's Eve, Grace had

Bette and Me

Above: View from the
front of the house.

Right: View from the
River Room.

Below: Bette's car.

Above: The sitting room.

Left: Oscars on the mantlepiece.

Below: Bette's bedroom.

Above: Bette, B.D., Ashley (aged six mon and me.

Left: B.D. with Ashley, aged eighteen months.

Above: Bette,
B.D. and
Michael.

Right: Margot
toasting her
mother.

Bette's favourite sofa,
surrounded by presents.

Opening the presents.

Michael and Vik Greenfield
looking on.

vin Bridges

With Michael and Margot.

A contented Bette, just about to serve the Christmas cold cuts at lunchtime. Goose would follow for dinner.

Michael fooling around.

Bette and her hats

Above: A cigarette in the dining room at the end of a day's work.

Right: This unusual Easter bonnet had an enormous pink bow on it.

invited us over for dinner to meet a friend of hers. However by early evening Twin Bridges was warm and cosy and Bette decided that she didn't want to venture out into the snow, so she rang Grace and suggested that she and her friend came over to Twin Bridges instead, and let Bette cook one of her favourite dishes – 'Chicken à la B.D.' – for them.

'But my friend has prepared a special pâté for you,' Grace protested.

'Bring the pâté with you,' replied Bette, and Grace gave in.

When they arrived, Grace's gentleman friend 'swished' through to the kitchen with an enormous silver platter of pâté, followed by Bette. A few minutes later she came storming out muttering, 'I'm so mad, I'm so mad! That man has taken over my kitchen. He's cutting my bread and ordering me around.' Five minutes later she reappeared from another direction. 'Jesus, I'm mad!' Everything was popping and her eyes were blazing. The unwitting guest had broken two cardinal rules: he had entered her kitchen and tried to take it over and, as a man, he was trying to serve Bette rather than letting her serve him.

The evening became very frosty indeed. Everyone ate so much pâté they didn't have room for the chicken and when, as they were leaving, the visitor tried to insist that we keep the rest of the pâté, Bette practically pushed it down his throat in her anxiety to be rid of both him and the offending food. Once they had gone, Bette paced up and down the house, seething with anger. Every Christmas she had a giant wreath on the door. It was minus five degrees outside and the leaves had become as crisp and dry as tobacco. She ripped it off the door and hurled it onto the sitting room fire. The flames came licking out of the fireplace and up the chimney. I thought we were about to see the whole house go up, but Bette was too absorbed in her fury to notice anything.

We were still up at three thirty in the morning when Margot appeared at the top of the stairs in her white nightdress, complaining that she was hungry. Instead of giving her some milk and cookies, Bette insisted that she came downstairs and the three of us solemnly sat down to eat her 'Chicken à la B.D.', which was an extremely rich concoction of chicken cooked in mushroom soup and flavoured with just about every herb that Bette could put her hands on! A couple of hours later I thought I was going to die!

Her next-door neighbour in Westport was a young woman called

Marsha, who had a very pleasant husband and young daughter. Vik told me a funny story one year about when Marsha went away on holiday. She had asked Bette to look after her tank of tropical fish but when Bette went round to feed them, she somehow managed to knock the whole box of fishfood into the tank. The fish, of course, continued to eat until they were dead, and Marsha returned to a beautiful, floating graveyard.

'Bette,' she stormed, 'you've killed my fish!'

'Nonsense,' Bette replied, without batting an eyelid, 'Vik did it.'

Although Vik would undoubtedly have shouldered the blame bravely, Marsha was not stupid and knew very well who the culprit was. Bette, however, could not abide being called a liar, even when she was one, so diplomatic relations were suspended for two years and any communication had to be done over the garden fence, through Marsha's daughter.

I don't believe Bette ever socialised with the other First Family of the area, the Newmans, although she always supported their various charities. I can remember we once passed Joanne Woodward in the town and her jaw dropped at the sight of Bette Davis on the street, just like any other star-struck housewife. The local tradespeople became very used to Bette. The grocery store used to send up her supplies, addressed to 'Betty Davis'.

I think this was probably one of the least turbulent times in Bette's troubled life. During the early part of our relationship, she had found a degree of stability with Vik at her side virtually all the time, and Peggy and I drifting in and out of her life. If only she could have held on to that fleeting piece of stability, maybe she could have ended up a great deal happier.

7
Christmas with Bette

Bette and I celebrated a couple of Christmases together, the first at Twin Bridges. It was a time of year that she loved, and she had very set ideas on how it should be run. There had to be two trees: one outside in the garden and another indoors, both with little fairy lights all over them. The outside one would go up about three days before Christmas, with poor Vik – who is completely useless at anything like that – and me wrestling with a giant ladder, all the lights and a fifteen-foot tree. Both of us would end up falling all over the place while Bette stood down below, hands on hips, legs apart, shouting instructions to us as we weaved and swung about in the branches. Bulbs were forever exploding. It was a nightmare, but the results were always beautiful.

Christmas Day always started the same way. We all had to eat 'gruel', like something from a genuine Dickensian Christmas story. It was a sort of porridge, unlike anything I had ever eaten before. The present-opening ceremony began at 10 a.m. after we had finished the 'gruel', and Bette had very set ideas on how it should be conducted. Each person had to open one present in turn. The only problem was that Bette received around seven hundred presents each year, while the rest of us had half a dozen. The result was that we always ended up watching her opening parcel after parcel. She did her best to even things up by sending Vik out to buy lots of little things for everyone else, but presents kept arriving for her every ten minutes during the fortnight before Christmas, and there was no way she could provide us with anything comparable.

She was ferocious about clearing up the waste paper as she went along. If you wanted to keep the label off something she had given to you, you had to be very quick off the mark or she would have swept it into the litter basket. One year she gave me a beautiful Canadian buckskin dressing case with my initials on, and I really wanted to be able to keep her gift tag inside the case but I turned away for a split second and it was gone. I had to hunt right through the rubbish later on to rescue it.

Bette kept a meticulous record of everything she received, so that she could write thank-you notes, and also so that she could ensure that she did not give a present back to somebody later by mistake. Many of the big stars operated what they called their 'boutiques'. Because they received so many presents from admirers and colleagues in the business, there was no chance that they could use them all so they would keep a store and use them as presents for other people at a later date. I remember Cary Grant sending Bette an enormous Fabergé Lemon, filled with their products. 'Oh my god, Fabergé!' she exclaimed on opening it. 'I hate it!'

One year Bette gave me a birthday gift from Neiman Marcus which absolutely delighted me. As I was opening it she danced around my seat, looking over my shoulder and biting her finger, sighing and making a major performance out of it. The gift was a little china dish in the shape of a heart, with a whistle inside. On the outside was the inscription 'If you ever need me, whistle'. I was delighted, even though it was one of Lauren Bacall's immortal lines, not one of Bette's. I had seen them in the shop and thought they were delightful.

'Are you sure you like it?' Bette asked anxiously.

'Bette, it's wonderful, I love it!' I assured her, but she still looked concerned.

'And you're sure you didn't give it to me?'

Bette didn't expect people to give her extravagant gifts. One year we went shopping together and she picked out a pair of imitation pearl earrings.

'You can buy me these for Christmas, Roy,' she announced.

'But they are only two dollars,' I protested.

'I want them. If Bette Davis wears these earrings, then they are real pearls.' I did as I was told and she often wore them.

One year I saw Bette more moved than I had ever seen her. Each Christmas B.D. gave her a new date book. They were nothing elaborate, just simple diaries bound in red board that Bette could fill with her jottings in red ink. One year B.D. wrote an inscription in the front, from an old Jewish proverb: 'Because God is so busy, he invented mothers.' Bette was moved to tears as she read it for the first time and throughout the day, every time she showed the present to someone else, she cried afresh. It was exactly the sort of message which she always wanted to hear from B.D.

Later on Christmas Day B.D. and Jeremy would come over, and Michael and Margot would be there. Sometimes Gary Merrill's brother and sister-in-law and their children were invited. Bette would insist on cooking the entire dinner herself, which one year was for twenty-one people in all and included two twenty-pound geese which had to be basted every fifteen minutes. It was like watching a miracle, seeing Bette's diminutive body dashing and spinning round the kitchen, trying to keep pace with everything that was going on.

She enjoyed having Christmas songs playing in the background – over and over again – and I must have heard Bing Crosby singing 'White Christmas' a thousand times in just one visit.

However toughly she acted, beneath the surface Bette was just as vulnerable with regard to her children, and just as anxious about them, as any other mother. One year the snow was particularly bad and Michael and his fiancée Chou had driven up to visit Michael's father Gary Merrill. They had gone in the MG sports car which Bette had bought for him in London with a little help from me. As the weather conditions became worse and the snow continued to fall, Bette telephoned Gary to tell him not to let the kids set out until the morning. She was too late, as they had already left. Bette was furious and instantly telephoned Chou's mother to have strong words with her as she had been the one who had instructed them to return. She was answered by the maid who told her that Chou's mother was out that evening, 'having dinner with Bette Davis'.

'That she is not,' she snarled, 'I am Bette Davis and she most certainly is not having dinner with me.'

When she eventually got hold of the woman she did not hold back. 'You may want your daughter dead,' she shouted, 'but I want my son alive! How could you force them to drive on a day like this?'

Later that night, while she was still fuming and pacing up and down, we received another call, from a rabbi. Apparently the car had 'blown up' outside his house and Michael and Chou were taking refuge with him.

'Could you send someone up to collect them?' the rabbi asked innocently.

This was the final straw. 'Send someone out on a night like this?' she screamed. 'I wouldn't send a dog out in this!'

She hung up and swung round on me. 'We're going to bed early,' she announced. 'I don't want to be up when Michael gets in.' Bette was actually extremely relieved to know they were safe after being at her wits' end with worry all day. Later that night Michael arrived and crept in to my room.

'How's mother?' he asked.

'How do you think she is, Michael?'

'What can I do, Roy?'

I thought for a moment. Bette's best time of the day was always first thing in the morning. If you ever wanted to ask her for anything, that was the time to do it. 'Try getting in before Vik with her morning coffee,' I suggested, 'and apologise.'

The next morning I heard him knocking on Bette's door and going in. I went to my bedroom door to listen.

'I've brought your coffee, mother,' he said. There was complete silence. 'I'm sorry about last night.' Still no response. 'Can I borrow your car today, to go and see Chou?' I waited for the explosion.

'Yes,' she said quietly and Michael emerged from the room, breathing a huge sigh of relief. Once he had gone I went in to her. She was sitting up with her coffee and early morning cigarette.

'Why on earth did you say he could have the car after all that?' I asked.

'What am I going to do, make him a prisoner in the house? He needs the car to visit his girl.' Once again I had seen that when something serious happened she was surprisingly magnanimous.

Most of my memories of Twin Bridges are snowbound. One year it was so bad, Bette and I were trapped together in the house for days, eventually living off frozen and tinned food, and getting to know one another even better. One morning she announced that she was going out to clear the bridges. I declined to join her, being comfortable in front of the fire. Americans love keeping their properties free from dirt and snow; they are forever clearing their lawns and driveways. I was curled up on Bette's chaise longue, browsing through her old scrap books, and I was not tempted to become part of the picturesque scene outside. She pulled on all her waterproofs, including a hat, and set out with a shovel and axe to clear the ice. A short while later I heard a squeaking of brakes and then Bette returned with icicles hanging from her nose because she was so cold, pulling off the sou-wester and tossing it aside.

'Now that's what I call something,' she told me.

'A truck driver pulled up and said: "Are you Bette Davis?" I replied: "That I am." He said: "May I have your autograph?" and I said: "That you may." '

'What's so extraordinary about that?' I asked.

'I was bending over,' she said. 'He could only have seen my ass.'

On one of these evenings, when it was literally several degrees below freezing, Bette and I were enjoying our usual cocktail hour, which was always the most delightful time of day when it was just the two of us. There was a loud bang on the back door. I went to see who it was and a rather superior young lady fell into the kitchen.

'I've lost my way,' she gasped, 'and I should be met by my boyfriend at the end of Crooked Mile, but I can't see a thing and I don't know where I am. Can I use your telephone?'

I told her to wait a minute and went to tell Bette what had happened. She could sometimes be rightly suspicious of people coming into the house. She said yes, of course the girl could use the 'phone. I went back and showed the girl where the wall 'phone was. She dialled her number and started to talk.

'I'm at the end of Crooked Mile,' she said. 'Please come and pick me up . . . How do I know where I am . . . I've fallen in the snow, it's deep . . .' She turned round and saw Bette standing in the doorway. Her mouth fell open and her words dried up. She was dumb-struck, but managed to stutter out the rest of her message before dashing from the house. Bette and I went back to our cocktails, when there was another knock at the door. I went back out and it was the girl again.

'I think I left my handbag,' she apologised and then leant close to me, 'was it. . . . ?'

'Yes,' I said.

'Oh, my goodness!' she cried, and fled back into the blizzard outside.

In 1970, Bette was in New York on the day before Christmas Eve, dubbing a film called *Bunny O'Hare* in a studio on Broadway. She suggested that I meet her in the studio and we could drive

59

out to Westport together. Watching Bette work at the highly skilled job of 'looping', was an education in itself. As they played the film a line ran across the bottom of the screen. Whenever it 'looped' Bette had to speak her lines in order to synchronise them with the lip movements on the screen. I doubt if anyone could have worked as fast and accurately as she did. The last line in the film, as she and Ernest Borgnine were driving off on a motorcycle, was for Ernest to say, 'What about the children?' and for Bette to reply, 'Fuck 'em.' The producers didn't think they could say 'fuck' for the British version, so they asked Bette to substitute the word 'screw'. Bette was adamant.

'There is no way I am going to say the word "screw" on screen,' she said. 'It is a dirty, filthy word and I will not say it.'

Everyone in the studio racked their brains and I suggested she say 'Bugger 'em', knowing that it would sound just as rude as 'screw 'em' to British ears, but doubting if Bette would realise it. I was right. She was quite happy to use the substitute word and it looped well. Then we were able to set off for Westport.

All through the day it had been snowing hard and Bette had been becoming progressively more anxious about getting home safely. We had all been trying to calm her down, but the weather conditions were becoming very bad. The studio had supplied us with a stretch limousine, the sort which burns a gallon of fuel a minute, and we ground to a halt in traffic on the Westport Turnpike. Bette is a nervous traveller anyway, but in the middle of a snowstorm she was nearly out of her mind. Nothing was moving anywhere, but the limo was gradually heating up. Bette became convinced that we would soon run out of fuel and we would be stranded beside the road in a snowdrift. She completely panicked, and was hanging out of the car shouting to passers-by: 'I'm Bette Davis. Take me to Westport.'

None of the other cars, of course, could move any faster than us, but she was convinced that the smaller vehicles were better equipped for the conditions. In the end the trip took us four hours when it should have taken one and Bette was nearly proved right. The chauffeur had just enough petrol to get himself down to the local gas station in time. Although I had started off trying to be a calming influence on Bette I had ended up being as panic-stricken as she was.

Another memorable Christmas was in London. Bette was to stay in one of the apartments at the Grosvenor House Hotel in Park Lane, with Peggy as her companion. Knowing that she liked a Christmas tree I went to the suite before she got there and set up a five-foot tree. When she arrived I received a call. She was thrilled and touched by the gesture, and insisted that my parents and I join them for dinner on Christmas Day.

As we drove there my father was very apprehensive, which always made him bad tempered, but he needn't have been. It was a perfectly delightful day. Bette was very warm and welcoming and we all had a wonderful time. I know because they used to joke about it that it had crossed my parents' mind that, however unlikely it might have seemed at the outset, they could well be in the company of a future daughter-in-law.

8

Oscars and Other Awards

Bette didn't like going to the Academy Award ceremonies but I loved them. To me they were the quintessential Hollywood, the most exciting, moving and glittering occasions. On the fiftieth anniversary of the Awards in 1978, however, she did agree to attend. It was to be one of the greatest and most historical events Hollywood had ever seen. She asked the famous columnist and broadcaster Robert Osborne to escort her. When I heard that she was going I couldn't believe it.

'Oh, Bette,' I said, 'I would do anything for a chance to go to the Oscars with you.'

'Of course you will,' she said and bought me an extra ticket, which is almost unheard of since everyone has two allocated to them and no more.

All the big names had agreed to come out that night: as well as Bette, there was Astaire, Stanwyck, Holden and de Havilland. What I really hoped was that we would be able to come in through the 'Walk of Fame', that strip of carpet which reaches from the stars' limousines into the front entrance of the Dorothy Chandler Pavilion with the fans and cameras crowded behind the barriers and the interviewer, Army Arched, trying to coax the stars up onto his platform to say a few words into his microphone. But Bette wasn't having any of that. Not only was she going to go in through a back entrance into the scene docks, but she was also going to stay backstage throughout the performance and she was going to plan her own route for the limousine.

On Oscar night the whole city is disrupted, and the police work out a very complex system of routes to get the stars safely to the door with the minimum of hold-ups for the traffic. Bette instructed her driver to take us against the one-way system in order to avoid the crowds. Who was he to argue with Bette Davis? A young policewoman, however, was furious, and stepped out in front of the car, blowing her whistle loudly. We stopped, the window glided down and she saw Bette Davis's face staring out at her. She jumped back with a start, dropping her whistle. The car glided forward, crushing it flat. I had by this time resorted to the contents of the in-car cocktail cabinet.

Once inside the building we made our way through the scene dock. Coming towards us we saw what appeared to be some sort of Amazonian tribe, in leather and chain outfits. As they passed, Bette stared after them in disbelief.

'Who was that?' she asked loudly.

'More a question of what was that?' I suggested.

Later in the evening we discovered that it was Diane Keaton, who was to win the Oscar that night for *Annie Hall*, and some friends.

We went on through to the Green Room and Bette sat down. After glancing round the room she beckoned me to bend down, and whispered in my ear.

'Who is this young man next to me?'

I looked. It was Jack Nicholson. It made me realise that even amongst the great, she is greater. No-one was looking at her and asking who she was. Everyone was lining up for the privilege of meeting and talking to her.

'I'm not missing this show,' I told her. 'Why don't you come out front with me?'

'No.' She waved me away. 'You go.'

I did, and revelled in every moment of it. That year two of the biggest names at the show were Bette Davis and John Travolta. She had survived long enough to be sharing the bill with someone who was young enough to be her grandson. I had actually introduced Bette and John before he became a star. It was at the Tony Awards a few years before, when two young performers asked me to introduce them to Bette. One was John, who was then a chorus boy, and the other was Bette Midler, who was an up-and-coming act, and who proceeded to tell us how she had been named after Bette Davis which did not please Miss Davis much.

The Tony Awards were held in New York at the Shubert Theatre that year and the police had closed off the whole of 44th Street because of the crowds. I had agreed to meet Bette at the theatre, but she decided to stop her limousine on Eighth Avenue and walk up a block. I couldn't believe my eyes when I saw what was approaching, and the people went wild. The tiny star (she is only five foot two) was walking through the crowds like a victorious Roman general returning home, flanked by policemen mounted on enormous horses.

The arrangements for the ceremony that year were in complete chaos. The Andrews Sisters were in residence at the theatre in *Over Here*, but there were no dressing rooms available for any of the other big names who turned up and nowhere for anyone to change. Henry Fonda was changing by a camera and Alice Faye was asleep by the stage, suffering from fatigue after flying into New York from the Mid-West where she was touring in *Good News*. I decided something had to be done, so I went to see Maxine Andrews and asked 'Are you going to allow anyone to share your dressing room?'

'Not on your life,' she replied cheerfully.

'Bette Davis?' I asked.

'Bring her up!'

So at least Bette had a room in which to dress and to meet her young admirers. She hadn't actually wanted to go to the Tony Awards that year, until she found out that Robert Preston was going to be there, and would be introducing her.

'My God,' she said when she heard the news, 'Robert Preston is the most under-rated talent Hollywood ever had. I have wanted to meet that man for years.'

At the same time Preston was being told that he was going to get the chance to introduce Bette Davis and he wrote a lyrical introduction for her, a eulogy which he delivered from the heart. When she came on, instead of going to her podium, she crossed straight over to him, got hold of his face and kissed him hard on the lips.

'I've been waiting to do that for years,' she announced to the astounded Preston and the astonished and loudly applauding audience.

Bette always knew how to stage-manage her appearance for the maximum effect. She was asked to present an award to Elizabeth Taylor during a tribute to the actress, which was being televised. She said 'yes', but only on the condition that there would be no announcement beforehand that she was going to do it. She did not want any rehearsals, she would simply appear. The request sounded like modesty, as if she did not want to steal any of

Elizabeth's thunder. Of course the exact opposite happened. When she walked out onto the stage unannounced the audience rose as one and cheered. The ovation seemed to last forever, and when poor Elizabeth came out her welcome, although warm, could not follow Bette's entrance.

Everyone in Hollywood wanted to pay homage to Bette all the time. After the 1978 Oscar ceremony which we attended together, we went on to the Governor's Ball at the Hilton, and I began to see why Bette had not wanted to sit in the front of the house during the Awards. All through dinner there was a permanent queue of people wanting to shake her hand and talk to her. They were serving lobster, which is her favourite, but she wasn't getting a chance to eat a single mouthful. Eventually I packed up her dinner and took her to the downstairs bar. In that darkened room I laid the food out for her and she was finally able to eat in peace.

The glory and glamour I felt I had missed on entering the Oscar ceremony, however, was nothing compared to that the year before, the night that Bette was given her Lifetime Achievement Award by the American Film Institute. This is one of the most prestigious awards that anyone in the industry can receive. Until then it had only been awarded to John Ford, James Cagney, Orson Welles and William Wyler.

The institute asked her to provide three new pictures of herself for publicity purposes. I had recently met George Hurrell, a charming, elderly man who had been one of the great photographers at Warners in the golden era of Hollywood. I told Bette I had met Hurrell and she immediately agreed that it would be a good idea to ask him if he would take the photographs. George came to my apartment at the Magic Hotel, bringing some of his old photos with him, including some early ones of Bette. He was delighted to have the chance to photograph Bette again and the resulting pictures were wonderful. Since then, his photographs have become collectors' items and he has published a book of his best work.

Another time, I arranged for Bette to sit for Vivienne, the great British portrait photographer, and the picture used on the front cover of this book was a gift from her to Bette and myself to express her gratitude. I also got Bette to sit for a drawing by Don Bachardy, and when he held his famous New York exhibition that picture was used on all the billboards and on the invitations, as a kind of logo.

For the AFI Award, Bette asked her old make-up man, Gene Hibbs, to come out of retirement and invited Peggy Shannon to do her hair.

As she entered the ballroom at the Beverly Hilton Hotel, the whole room stood to applaud. Like ripples on a pond the applause continued until Bette's diminutive figure disappeared in the sea of applauding, cheering bodies. These were people in the industry, not just fans, and they roared and shouted, they stamped and hollered their tribute to the lady who could realistically be called 'Queen of Hollywood'. It was like a glorious dream to share an evening like this, which was a culmination of her entire life's work, with Bette Davis, who was now recognised by everyone in the industry as the greatest screen actress of all time. Just a few hours before I had been watching her in the kitchen, writing her speech. They may not have been applauding me, but they were applauding my friend. I certainly felt very proud of her.

There were speeches from many of the people she had worked with throughout her career, including Olivia de Havilland, looking rather large in a beautiful Christian Dior dress.

'As a little girl in San Francisco,' she said, 'I remember looking at the screen and seeing this wonderful actress, Bette Davis. Now, two Oscars later, I come to pay tribute.'

Later Bette also made a speech: 'This is the icing on the cake of my career. I am truly overcome. In 1926, from Lowell Massachusetts, came Ruth Elizabeth Davis, known as Bette, who was not beautiful, not tall and willowy, who had a tiny voice that couldn't be heard past the first row of the theatre. She didn't know whether she had talent, but she did have drive and ambition.'

To Bette's delight, William Wyler also spoke. He remembered the fight they had had over how their film *The Letter* should end. Bette had walked off the set in anger, but ended up doing it Wyler's way.

'If tonight I brought up the subject of that last scene,' he said, 'Bette would insist on going back to the studio and reshooting it the way she wanted.'

We were all up until two in the morning, before I made my way home. At nine o'clock the next morning I was awakened by the 'phone. I groped for it with my eyes shut and Bette's voice rang in my ears.

'What do you think of that?' she shouted. 'Olivia saying she remembered watching me as a kid. I told you she hated me.'

'Bette,' I said, 'Olivia is all of seven years younger than you.'

Although Bette has had honours heaped upon her, she has not received as many Oscars as she would have liked. From ten nominations she has only actually received two awards. One was for *Dangerous* (1935), which the Academy was probably giving her as a belated reward for *Of Human Bondage* (1934), which had failed to win the year before, and the other was for *Jezebel* (1938). Being a double Oscar winner put her amongst the crème de la crème for many years, but then Ingrid Bergman won a third for best supporting actress in *Murder on the Orient Express*, and that jangled Bette's nerves. Katharine Hepburn then won two in a row, giving her a total of four (even though one was shared with Barbra Streisand), and that made Bette begin to feel left behind.

Although it is her boast that the industry 'liked her', and although Hollywood always felt unable to deny her talent, it seems that they didn't like her all that much, and as she became progressively more unpleasant and difficult to work with they began to actually dislike her. Although she was the first woman to be honoured by the AFI, she has never been awarded a 'Special Oscar', which her body of work certainly merits. She has had bad luck in that she has missed a number of parts which won Oscars for the actresses that played them, such as *A Streetcar Named Desire* – which she turned down – and *Who's Afraid of Virginia Woolf* – which she fought for and lost – but had she been easier to work with she probably would have been offered more of the really good parts, and could have extended her run at the top. There have also been parts like Margot Channing in *All About Eve* (1950) which definitely deserved an award. Although they applauded her talent, few of her peers seem able to love her as a person, and so they do not vote her the honours she deserves so much.

9
Hollywood Days

At the beginning of our relationship I warned Bette that I was an enormous fan of her work, knowing that often she found the adoration of fans rather too cloying for everyday life.

'What are we going to do about it?' I asked. 'I'm going to want to ask you endless, trivial questions about the old Hollywood movies and studios.'

She thought for a moment. 'All right,' she said, 'we will make Wednesdays Hollywood Days. We will talk about Hollywood as much as you like on Wednesdays.'

She was as good as her word, answering every question I had about every minor star she had ever played with, analysing and assessing all her own performances and those of her peers. Each time she had new publicity pictures taken she would write a message across one and let me have it for my collection.

For a devoted admirer of hers, however, just being with Bette was enough, because privileged moments were always occurring when I was able to actually live out some of the scenes which I remembered so vividly from her films. At the end of a hard day's shooting, coming into her dressing room, I would find her with her face smeared in cold cream, a drink in hand and her hair pushed back from her forehead, and it was like walking into her opening scene in *All About Eve*. All too often we had to 'fasten our seat belts'. At moments when she was behaving like a petulant little girl it was like being in the room with Baby Jane. Sometimes the lines between reality and fantasy become so confused that even the actors themselves get swept away in it. Bette once explained to me why she had married Gary Merrill:

'We met when we were filming *All About Eve*,' she explained. 'I was Margot Channing and he was my director Bill Sampson. We fell in love with each other in the film and in real life. We then got married in real life. But he thought he was marrying Margot and I thought I was marrying Bill. It wasn't long before he found out that I wasn't Margot, and he was certainly no Bill Sampson.'

Once a fan always a fan, and there are many of us. Director Bryan Forbes is the same, and I once jokingly told him that I would swap him Bette Davis for Katharine Hepburn. He agreed and I persuaded Bette to accompany me to his bookshop in Virginia Water, Surrey, to sign some copies of books and send them off as Christmas presents. I had actually forgotten about the bargain I had made when one day, while I was at the Forbes's house, Katharine Hepburn rang. Bryan said, 'Would you like to talk to her?' and handed over the 'phone. For at least ten minutes she told me about all the problems she was having on her current film *The Prime of Miss Jean Brodie* and then the line went dead. I was delighted to have had a chance to hear the voice speaking to me and hung up. A few minutes later it rang again. Bryan picked it up.

'It's Katharine. I was talking to Roy and I got cut off. . . .' I took the receiver back and she went on talking for another twenty minutes about how she had been fired from the film and how George Cukor had offered to resign but she had told him to keep working with her replacement, Maggie Smith (who later received an Oscar for the part).

My greatest thrill however came at Laguna Beach, and was beautifully staged by Bette. Laguna is a pretty little resort town just south of Los Angeles. Bette and her third husband, William Grant Sherry (B.D.'s father), had lived there when they were married, and Bette's cousins the Favors were still there. She often went down to stay with them and I would visit her.

John and Sally Favor were a charming couple, with a pleasant house in the Laguna Hills. When 'Cousin Bette' came to stay she was given a small room at the back of the house, and it was during one of these stays that she wrote her commentary for the book *Mother Goddamn!*. It was a book in which the facts of her career were written by Whitney Stine, and Bette made comments in the margins in red ink. She used to work on the pages in Laguna and I would take them up to Stine in Los Angeles when I returned in my car.

One day she and I went out for a walk about town. She wanted to buy a swimming costume and a few other things so we started to browse around the shops. In each shop, the assistants would

greet her like an old friend and word spread down the street that
Miss Davis was in town. When we reached the swimwear store
she went into a cubicle to try on a costume, and when she came
out the store was packed with people wanting to see her. She loved
it, sitting cross-legged on the floor signing autographs and chatting
with old friends. When we eventually escaped from the crowd, we
looked down across the beach, and she pointed to a building up
on the cliffs above us.

'That's where we are going to eat tonight,' she said, 'Victor
Hugo's.'

'Great,' I said, and walked on.

'No,' she grabbed my arm, 'Look at it. It's going to be special.'

She wouldn't say any more than that and I was intrigued. That
evening we drove up to the restaurant, and as we walked in we
received the usual, head-turning welcome. Bette, however,
marched me to the side of the restaurant and out onto the balcony,
where it was blowing a minor gale, to the amazement of staff and
diners alike.

'Look at the view,' she smiled.

'Very nice,' I agreed, looking out over the palm trees to the bay
and the coast.

She looked at me intensely. 'Light me, Roy,' she said eventually,
and I realised what she had done. She had brought me to the
exact location which was used in her film *Now Voyager!* for the
famous scene where Paul Henreid lights two cigarettes and passes
one to her. It was a scene which set a romantic fashion all over
the world, and has become a classic of movie history. Unfortunately, Bette had forgotten how early the nights fall in California
and how cold they can sometimes be. With our hair whipped by
the wind, and the chilled breezes coming in from the sea, I did as
she asked, and relived for real one of my great cinematic
experiences.

All through her career Bette was an idol of the gay community.
They were part of the hardcore of fans who would go anywhere to
see her in anything, whether it was a lecture or a play, a film or
a television pot-boiler. When she was appearing in *Night of the
Iguana* by Tennessee Williams, she would find the stage door
crowded with men wanting her autograph, and asking just to see
her. She didn't understand why this happened. I tried to explain
that married couples were less likely to come backstage because if

the man was the fan the woman would probably be wanting to get home, or if she was the fan her husband might well not be interested. The single people, however, had the freedom to do just what they wanted, and they wanted to show their love for her.

Yet she often made very anti-gay remarks, and I had to remind her that these people were her most loyal followers. She was very puzzled by the nature of homosexuality and would often ask me, 'But what exactly do they do, Roy?'

I would explain as best I could but I don't think she really understood. I do believe, however, that she eventually came to appreciate just how important her gay fans were to her. One particular incident will always live in my memory. An old friend of Bette's, the film actress Geraldine Fitzgerald, was giving a folk-singing concert at The Backlot in Los Angeles. The Backlot at Studio One is part of a gay complex, and has a cabaret room that people can rent for shows. Bette agreed, reluctantly, to introduce Geraldine since she was a good friend, and word got around that Bette was going to be there.

The club, as its name implies, is situated on a backlot on Robertson, off Santa Monica Boulevard in West Hollywood, and can only be reached by a fire escape. It is, however, immensely large and hugely popular. That night it was packed to the rafters, and a lot of star names had also turned out. Kirk Douglas, Roger Moore, Olivia de Havilland, Paul Henreid and Gregory Peck were all there. I didn't believe that they had come to hear Geraldine sing. They were there to see Bette in action again. The crowd of celebrities meant that many of the gays, whose club it was, weren't able to get into the room, which made Bette and me angry.

John Houseman introduced Bette, who nearly broke her neck falling down the steps onto the stage in order to announce Geraldine. Geraldine sang for about ninety minutes – a medley of Irish folk songs – and when she finished, she called for a package to be brought on stage.

'I've searched everywhere,' she said, 'to find a present for Bette Davis,' and she proceeded to make the most generous tribute to Bette and explained how the great star had helped her when she had found herself working with her on her first film *Dark Victory* (1939). 'I had been warned that this great actress would upstage me every minute,' she said. 'I was advised to wedge myself in between pieces of furniture so that Miss Davis wouldn't be able to manoeuvre me out of camerashot. I did as they suggested and Miss Davis looked at me as if I was mad. She was actually the most generous of actors.' Geraldine then produced a paperweight, which she had had made to represent the world.

'Bette, this is for you because I think the world of you. You are the world,' and she sent it over to our table via one of the waiters. Bette leapt to her feet, pushing past the waiter in her rush to the stage, tripped down the steps onto the stage once more and hugged and kissed Geraldine like a long-lost sister.

When the show was over and it was time for us to leave, we had to walk down a long narrow passage, which was lined, on both sides, by men from the club who just wanted to be near to her, to talk to her, and to have her brush against them. Outside they were lining both sides of the fire escape, and they all stretched out their arms to form two human balustrades like a wild idea from a Busby Berkeley musical. She descended to the ground like the queen that she was to all of them, passing from one arm to the next. As she passed, their voices set up a steady murmur in the night air:

'You're great.'

'You're gorgeous.'

'We love you.'

It was true hero-worship, and by the time we had reached the limousine, a crowd had gathered which was so thick that we were unable to get through, all of them chanting their adorations. When we finally managed to get the door of the car open and force her inside, I was unable to follow. I could hear her shouting through the crowd, 'Get in the car, Roy! Roy, quickly, get in!', but it was impossible.

At that time she only lived a few blocks away, so I walked after her, arriving back fifteen minutes later. When I walked into the kitchen she pulled off her wig and slumped down with a groan.

'Thank God that is over!'

I was furious with her. 'If you don't want to enjoy that,' I snapped, 'I'm going to bask in your reflected glory. That was one of the most moving moments I have ever witnessed.'

I believe that when she came to think about it, she had to agree that she was moved. At times she became so adept at treating the art of being a star as 'just a job', that she allowed some of the magical moments to escape her.

She was always excessively nosey about other people's private lives, including the gay community, and got a great kick out of listening in to rows. There were two men living next door to her Hollywood apartment, and she discovered that if they both had their windows open she could hear all their arguments – of which there were plenty. When these men found out they had Bette Davis for a neighbour they could hardly contain their excitement, and she happily visited them for dinner.

One of the men was tall and handsome, while the other was the exact opposite. To start with Bette always took the side of the good-looking one in arguments. One day, however, she had made them a chocolate cake for one of their birthdays. At least she told me she had made it. Anyway, an enormous row broke out between the two men which eventually overflowed into her apartment. The little one came running in, in floods of tears, and threw himself into Bette's arms, sobbing. 'Oh, he's so terrible to me!' She wanted to take the handsome one's part, but suddenly the door flew open again and he came in, grabbed his boyfriend out of Bette's arms, pushed her aside, threw her chocolate cake back at her and asked her not to interfere. There was nothing Bette liked more than a good domestic fight. She pulled the ugly one back to her bosom, telling him not to worry because she was protecting him now. From then on she never had a good word to say for her former favourite.

Bette was sometimes accused of being a fag hag, particularly by her husband Gary Merrill. The problem was that because she was such a strong and dominating personality, she often made heterosexual men feel threatened. Gay men posed no threat to her, and were quite willing to let her think she dominated them.

It is also interesting that she was so attractive to strong women. When we were discussing the subject of lesbianism once she thought about it for a while and said; 'If I woke up to find two big boobs in bed beside me, I would die!'

The gay movement in California, however, was always looking for star names to endorse its cause. While Bette thought that they had done good work in the early days at bringing the issue of homosexuality out of the closet, she did not want to become one of their champions.

While she was touring California she appeared at the Long Beach Civic Auditorium in her one-woman show. At the time there was a scandal about some school teachers being dismissed when it was discovered they were homosexuals. One of the men in the audience asked her to make a statement on where she stood on the issue.

Bette strode to the front of the stage. 'Why don't you people just shut up?' she snapped. 'Shut up, shut up, shut up!'

She believed that the whole issue had gone far enough and that they had made their point effectively.

10
London, 1971

In the 1970s the National Film Theatre in London held a long series of lectures sponsored by John Player, the tobacco company, at which great stars and directors would sit in front of an audience to talk about their careers and answer questions. I had already arranged for Olivia de Havilland to give one. The organisers were desperate to persuade Bette to appear, but weren't able to get to her. They approached me and asked if I could talk her into it.

I thought it would be a brilliant idea, and I suggested to Bette that she should let me organise it. To start with I don't think she appreciated how many people would want to come to hear her talk but eventually she agreed. A week before the event, however, she started playing up. She was filming *Madame Sin* on location in Scotland and she rang me.

'I don't think I will be able to make it,' she said. 'I think I'd like to drive back and take in the scenery.'

'Okay, Bette.' I stayed calm although I was seething. 'We'll just run *All About Eve* without you and have a good time.'

There was no way I could have done that, since the BBC were going to televise the appearance. She kept ringing me back but I refused to take her calls for a few days.

Finally I spoke to her and she was as sweet as pie. 'I've decided to fly down instead of driving, so I shall be back at the Berystede [the hotel in Sunninghill where she was staying during the filming]. Book a room for yourself, come down and we'll have a really nice weekend. Then we can drive up to London together.'

I was relieved at her change of attitude. I did as she said and agreed to meet her at the hotel at four o'clock on the Friday afternoon. I then made sure I didn't get there until about seven in the evening. Bette was going mad, ringing my parents and everyone else she could think of to find out where I was.

The Berystede is a large hotel in a beautiful setting, and the sort of place where young couples go for 'romantic weekends'. When I finally drew into the car park I found all these people standing in groups, staring up at a third-floor window in a turret at the front of the hotel. I looked up and there, at the window, was the Bette Davis face. She was hanging out of her window, watching for me. All through the car park I could hear them whispering her name to one another.

'Come straight up!' she shouted to me, since I always made a point of announcing myself at reception when I was visiting her in hotels. I went straight up, and the grim face was waiting for me. 'I've brought you a present. I've hidden it. You've got to find it.' I guessed she had put it in the ice bucket so I went straight there – which didn't please her – and found a lovely pair of cufflinks.

Eventually she thawed out and the weekend started to go well but that evening, while we were watching her film *Winter Meeting* on television, she passed out on the bed. I didn't realise what had happened at first. I took the cigarette out of her fingers before it set light to the hotel and then I decided that she was too still to be simply asleep. I tried to awaken her, beginning to panic. I put my face to her nostrils to see if she was still breathing, I shouted at her, banged cupboard doors and did everything I could to awaken her.

After what seemed like hours she snapped awake. 'What's the matter?' she asked, completely unaware that anything was wrong. Could it have been a kind of nervous reaction to stress? I don't know to this day.

Anyhow, the response to the lecture was fantastic. Bette chose Max Factor in Bond Street to do her make-up. As the lecture was being held on a Sunday, they agreed to open their arcade premises specially, which involved getting the permission of all the other shops in the arcade to open the gates. By the time we reached the National Film Theatre, crowds were lining the streets.

Bette had asked to have Joan Bakewell as her interviewer, which I thoroughly approved of. Before the day I had rehearsed with Joan, playing Bette's part myself, in order to ensure a smooth flow on the night. Joan and I agreed never to tell Bette that we had held a mock run-through without her, knowing that she wanted the event to be spontaneous. Joan, however, was grateful for the rehearsal.

I also suggested to Bette that she make her entrance from the back of the theatre and walk through the audience instead of appearing from the 'wings' – actually a door at the side of the stage. It was the first time this had been done. The audience loved her and gave her a massive standing ovation when she reached the stage and again when she finally left the cinema. As she made her way to the stage she was enveloped by the audience, all of whom left their seats to speak to her and shake her hand. It was a wonderful welcome.

We played a number of her film clips, one of which was a present from me to Bette. It was a rare clip of her singing and dancing, 'You're Either Too Young or Too Old' from *Thank Your Lucky Stars*, which was nearly always cut out when the film was shown on television in America. It was usually run late at night and was a long film, with her appearance somewhere in the middle. Fans handling prints of the film had stolen the famous scene years before, so she hadn't seen it for decades. I had managed to get hold of a copy. She was delighted by the surprise, crowing with laughter on stage.

She thoroughly enjoyed the whole event and afterwards she said she would spend just ten minutes in the Green Room talking to members of the audience. I decided not to allow any celebrities backstage that night because I wanted her to be completely alone with her fans, and both she and they loved it. When I came into the room she had kicked off her shoes and was sitting cross-legged on the floor talking to everyone. She stayed there for an hour and a half.

As we came out of the theatre afterwards, the crowds had swelled to uncontrollable numbers. Like the night at The Backlot in Hollywood it seemed impossible that we would ever get her to her Rolls Royce. In the end I picked her up bodily and carried her to it. As she went, she said she would sign copies of books about her, so I was standing behind her, with my arms around her middle, lifting her feet off the ground and moving towards the car, while she signed everything that was pushed at her, holding the pen at arm's length as she always did. I saw that one man was holding out a piece of paper which already had Ingrid Bergman's and Olivia de Havilland's autographs on it. I knew what she would do, because I had seen it before – she wrote Bette Davis right across the other two names. She never liked to share a page with anyone else.

At last we got into the car, but the pressure of the crowds on the car door had damaged it hopelessly and the driver had to stop a mile down the road and fasten it up with rope in order to get her back to her hotel safely.

This was the first of Bette's one-woman 'chat' shows, and she took to the idea so strongly that they turned into a tour in Britain and America, pulling capacity crowds at every stop. Bette was so pleased to have been asked to do the NFT event that she wouldn't even allow me to collect her appearance fee for her, which was disappointing since I was hoping to claim a percentage of it to cover my own expenses.

Her British tour was organised for her by Billy Marsh, a well-known variety agent whom I had worked with at the beginning of my career with the Bernard Delfont organisation. For some reason, he seemed to dislike me intensely. Mr Marsh's relationship with Bette was soured at the beginning when he told her that while she was playing the Palladium the upper circle would be closed, implying that Bette couldn't pull a crowd large enough to fill the theatre. Bette said she wouldn't appear unless all the 3000 seats were filled for all three performances. With her name, of course, it was not hard to sell the seats several times over.

When I went backstage after the second performance, one of Mr Marsh's henchmen forbade me entry and was grotesquely rude. The stage door keeper, who knew me well, was extremely surprised. The henchman did not realise that Bette always supplied doormen with lists of people to be admitted to her dressing room, written in red in her own handwriting. I heard someone say 'We don't want Roy Moseley in here,' but I knew the Palladium too well, and the Palladium knew me too well, for anyone to be able to keep me out of the lovely theatre where I had first worked in the West End. When I reached Bette's dressing room she was delighted to see me. She entertained a stream of visitors that night. Glenda Jackson was there with her strange, silent sister who merely sat in the middle of the room in a large armchair. Peter O'Toole and James Mason arrived and Danny La Rue. Bette did not like drag acts and had told me that she had been to see Danny at his club many years ago and greatly resented the way he proceeded straight onto first name terms with her – a habit he is famous for.

She was, however, cordial to him and his entourage that night. Jessie Matthews also arrived, proclaiming herself to be an undying fan of Bette's.

'I'm an actress as well,' Jesse explained, holding out a picture of Bette. 'I wondered if I could have your autograph?'

'Of course I know who you are,' Bette assured her, taking the photograph from her. 'Now is Matthews with one 't' or two?'

During the tour Bette had the help of a man called Jim Bronson. Jim was an inspired choice for the job of moving around the audience with a microphone, directing Bette towards her questioners. He was a charming, good-looking man, and Bette told me she fancied him.

One of the questions at the Palladium was: 'Miss Davis, you have often admitted that you had one great love in your life. Would you tell us who that was?'

'That I will not,' Bette answered.

'If I was to mention a name, would you tell me if I'm right?' the questioner persevered. 'Would it be Mr William Wyler?'

Bette smiled, but said nothing.

'Miss Davis, is that your own hair?' asked the next questioner, pointing at the vividly striped wig on her head.

Without blinking, Bette glared out at him. 'This is my own hair, my own eyes, my own teeth and my own boobs!' she replied, enjoying her own 'ballsy' approach.

One of the problems with the question and answer format is that there are always some film buffs in the audience who insist on droning on about pedantic details.

'Miss Davis,' said one, 'in *Now Voyager!* you come back into the house in the dark. The 'phone is ringing. It is Mr Henreid calling from the station to say goodbye. You turn on a lamp by the 'phone. It was an exceptionally bright light. Could you comment on this?'

'So I turned on a lamp, what do you mean?'

'It was exceptionally bright.'

'Then it must have been a damn bad shot,' she snapped and moved quickly on to the next question.

During this period Bette was persuaded to make a musical record with Norman Newell, an elderly producer who was putting a lot of stars on record for posterity. It was a sad idea since when it comes to singing Bette hasn't got a note. It was in fact one of the worst records ever made, although it has since become something of a collectors' item. Bette herself took over the marketing in America, and in one instance she signed hundreds of copies in a gay record shop in West Hollywood. Just after she had recorded this, I visited her at her apartment in the Grosvenor House. Norman Newell had brought her a tape but no-one had a recorder. I offered to pop home for mine.

'Yes, Roy,' sneered Billy Marsh from the corner of the room. 'Go get your tape recorder.'

I said nothing and duly obliged and we all listened to this bad recording which Bette thought was marvellous. That evening Mr Marsh was openly hostile to me again, and took no trouble to hide his chagrin when I finally showed him to the door.

One of the aspects of the tour which pleased Bette the most was the broad age range of the audience. We conducted a poll and found that their average age was only early twenties. There was one girl, aged twenty-two, who turned up at every single performance. She finally made herself known to Bette, giving her a charming present. Bette was delighted that such young people should be so interested and knowledgeable about her work. I was amazed, one evening during the tour, to arrive in Bette's hotel room and find one of the two single beds there completely covered in letters. They were all from fans and admirers, every one of them something which the ordinary person would treasure. Bette took great pains to answer them all personally.

When you become close to someone very famous, spending a lot of time alone with them in private homes, it is easy to forget just how unusual their situations are. It is only when you go out with them in normal public situations, that you begin to realise just how far from reality their lives have become. Because many of her greatest films were made a long time ago, and because she never bothered to dress like a Hollywood star, Bette was not always instantly recognisable to people. Often in the street or in shops, she would be treated as just another rather tiresome lady, until someone would realise who she was. The voice always gave her away. Then you would see their attitudes change completely. It must be said that Bette always tried to disguise her features by wearing little make-up and much less lipstick, and by wearing one of her famous 'caps'. She would dress very casually when she didn't want to be recognised, and wear dark glasses.

In one old-fashioned draper's shop in Sunninghill, Berkshire, she was being served by a particularly ill-tempered woman, the sort that never bothers to look at customers' faces anyway. I dare say Bette was being slightly difficult, asking to see a lot of things and not making her mind up instantly, but the woman was also being extremely brusque and impatient. While all this was going on, I noticed that a junior assistant had suddenly realised who it was being given this bad treatment, and was trying to attract her colleague's attention to warn her. The older woman steadfastly refused to respond to the 'Pssts' which the other woman was sending in her direction, but eventually agreed, with extremely bad grace, to go behind the scenes for a private word with her. When she emerged she was transformed with smiles and anxiety to please, and proceeded to fawn over Bette with an endless stream of 'Yes madam, certainly madam, anything you want madam, a pleasure to have you in our shop madam.' Bette bought a cheap nylon nightdress and assorted nylon scarves and, as she left with her purchases, let out a stage whisper to the effect that she had no intention of going back there again.

Fruiterers who displayed their goods outside their shops also tended to be upset by the sight of a dramatic-looking lady picking up a bit of this and a bit of that, and popping it all into her mouth to taste. At one such shop in Virginia Water a horrified young male assistant came rushing out to protest.

'You can't do that!' he shouted.

'Why not?' Bette asked, with genuine astonishment.

The young man was about to explain when a girl came chasing out after him, whispered hurriedly in his ear, and they both stood there grinning.

I don't think Bette ever really appreciated that she couldn't do whatever she wanted in life. One pleasant spring day we were walking down a country lane together when she spotted a particularly pretty garden. Jumping over the wall she began admiring the flowers and then dancing across the lawn. The family, who were sitting enjoying a Sunday lunch, were dumbstruck at this sight. Eventually the father leapt to the window and shouted at her to get off his property. I sometimes wonder what he would have done if he had known just who it was behaving like Isadora Duncan in his front garden.

Peggy Shannon told me of one of Bette's visits to her house, which co-incided with Halloween. Bette insisted on dressing up in a witch's hat and red wig and going 'trick or treating' in the neighbourhood. It was eight-thirty at night and people would answer their doors to her knocking, saying 'We have no more candy left.' Bette, however, had a huge basket full of the stuff and she would throw handfuls of it into the houses. None of the neighbours had any idea who she was. The next day Peggy heard a group of kids talking about the witch who had visited their houses to throw candy.

Getting through airports can also be a problem for stars, since it is easy for them to get trapped. On one arrival in Britain I met Bette off the plane and we were walking fast through the empty corridors to get out to the car. A cleaning lady looked up from her mopping and saw who was approaching at full speed. Letting out a cry of astonishment and pleasure, the woman rushed forward dropping her mop, which became entangled between her legs and hit Bette head first in the stomach. Film star and cleaner ended up in a tangle of limbs on top of a pile of cases. Although she was winded and surprised, Bette remained good-natured and the woman got her autograph.

Stars also have to spend a great deal of time away from their homes, either staying in other people's houses or in hotels, and as I've explained Bette liked to turn the hotels she stayed in into homes. I can remember driving down to visit her in one of the exclusive country hotels in Britain which she particularly liked. As I drew into the car park I saw a lady on her hands and knees in the flowerbeds, pulling up weeds – and some of the flowers as well. It was only as I got closer I realised it was Bette.

'What on earth are you doing?' I asked.

'Gardening,' she responded, as if it was the most natural thing in the world for a hotel guest to be doing.

One evening at the Berystede Hotel, Bette and I were descending the stairs to dinner. As we approached the reception area we heard a raised voice. There was a woman berating the young girl behind the desk.

'But I am a star!' she was boasting. 'I am an opera singer. I am here to do the cabaret; you must find me a dressing-room.'

As she drew level with the desk Bette smiled sweetly at the receptionist. 'Good evening.'

'Good evening, Miss Davis,' replied the startled girl. Swinging round to see who was interrupting her, the 'star' turned bright red, and Bette had succeeded in terminating the row.

At dinner we were seated next to a large man whose table manners left something to be desired. He appeared to be polishing off the entire cheese board. He immediately began to get on Bette's nerves and she started to make loud comments about how disgusting he was. I was becoming very disturbed, expecting him to come over and hit me at any moment, but fortunately he was too engrossed with his food to hear anything that was being said at a neighbouring table. When we had finished eating we went outside for a walk around the hotel. As we passed an open window we heard someone singing. It was the 'star' from reception, entertaining a small private party. She was trilling away 'I Could Have Danced All Night'. The curtains behind the singer were drawn back to allow some air into the room.

'Put your face to the window, Bette,' I suggested, 'just for a second.'

'I couldn't do that,' she protested. 'Oh, all right.'

A startled audience were suddenly treated to a glimpse of one of the most famous faces in the world over the shoulder of the singer, and then it disappeared as we both ran off into the night, giggling like naughty schoolchildren. Bette could be enormous fun to be with.

Despite her reputation, Bette was always immensely approachable to her fans. She never refused an autograph as long as there weren't huge crowds of people, and she always liked to give them a little show. Often autograph hunters would ask, 'Please could you inscribe it to . . . [whomever].'

Bette would then give her most sweeping 'Bette Davis' act barking: 'I don't put "to" I put "for"!' Grammatically, of course, she was correct.

One year she was staying at the Great Fosters hotel, a fine Elizabethan country house. As her car swept into the drive there was a gaggle of autograph hunters waiting outside. It was raining so Bette went straight in but a few minutes later she sent someone out to say that if they would like to send their books in, she would sign them. The autograph hunters said that they would rather wait until they could see her personally and continued to stand in the rain. Some hours later, as Bette came out to go to dinner, they approached her. She told them she had been watching them out of the window and thought they were mad to have waited so long, and she started signing for them. One young man gave her his pen, and it leaked ink over the gloves she was carrying.

'Look what you've done to my gloves!' came the Bette Davis cry, in a voice of mock fury.

Even casual encounters with Bette Davis were always dramatic. When in London with Gary Merrill one year, she went to the BBC to give an interview on the famous radio programme 'In Town Tonight'. When the couple emerged from the building afterwards, there were two Rolls Royces waiting by the pavement and a large crowd of fans. Bette climbed into the front Rolls and sat staring straight forward as the crowd pressed against the windows from the pavement. She waited for what seemed like an eternity until an official from the BBC poked his head in the window.

'Excuse me, Miss Davis,' he said, 'but you are in the wrong car, Mr Merrill is waiting in the second car.'

Unable to get out on the pavement side, Bette swept open the door on the road-side without a second glance, just as a cyclist was pedalling past, with his head down. The cycle hit the door, the cyclist went over the top and landed on the ground at Bette's feet. Without looking down, Bette pulled her coat around her, stepped over the prone body and strode imperiously to the second car. It was a classic Bette Davis moment, a vignette performance for the assembled crowd. I hasten to add that the man was not hurt.

The most melancholy picture which I have of these outings, however, was of Bette standing in a small local cinema, asking the surly assistants in the box office what was playing. None of them realised that they were actually talking to the first lady of the industry in which they were such humble minions, and they treated her with exactly the same sort of contempt with which these people treat all their customers, and which must be a contributary, if minor, factor to the sad closure of so many cinemas in Britain and America. Bette feigned amusement about this incident, but I could tell that she was disturbed.

11

The Men in her Life

Bette and I talked a lot about sex and marriage. When I first met her she told me that as far as sex was concerned she had 'zipped up'. As our relationship developed we became very relaxed together. There were never any locked doors in the house and she was happy to have me in her bedroom at most times.

She had always had a fondness for dark, 'five-o'clock shadow' men and I am certainly one of those, having had to shave twice a day since I was a teenager. She also told me that I reminded her of the young William Wyler, the famous director who was undoubtedly the love of her life. This was a considerable compliment and I only wish that I had a small part of Mr Wyler's talent. I am not a handsome man but then Bette, and most of the other great women of Hollywood, seldom went for the traditionally good-looking men. I am of average height, but that still meant I was able to rest my chin on the top of the diminutive Bette's head.

I have always been attracted to strong – which often means older – women. Bette, in her book *This 'n That*, confesses that she liked younger men: 'I've usually fallen in love with men younger than I – older men are so settled in their ways. Our society does not yet accept the older woman who marries the younger man, she is laughed at behind her back. It is one of the more curious taboos, when you consider that women stay sexually young much longer than men.'

Bette and I had so many interests in common that there were never any awkward gaps or silences when we were together. Both of us, for instance, were obsessed with her talents and career, and we could talk about them endlessly. I soon discovered that Bette liked to romanticise things, particularly incidents from her own past, which is why both the books she wrote are worthless as documents of reference. We both had a great love of America, of home life, of theatre and cinema. We liked the same sort of people, and we liked going to the same sort of places.

I believe there were opportunities when she was willing to 'unzip' sexually for me but I didn't take advantage of them. When she challenged me about why that was, I was able to answer very clearly.

'If I did, Bette, I wouldn't last ten minutes as your friend,' I explained, 'and I want our friendship to last as long as possible.'

There is no question that I loved her, and I found her devastatingly attractive right up till the end. She always had lovely legs, and was always groomed and turned out exactly as I like a woman to look. Apart from a rather low-slung bosom, she had kept her body in good shape. She went through a period of wearing a variety of wigs which Peggy Shannon created for her. The wigs themselves were brilliant creations, but they did nothing for Bette's face. She always looked loveliest with her own baby hair.

If I had become her lover there might well have been financial advantages. I would, for instance, have been able to ask her to pay for my flights back and forth across the Atlantic, and many other things. I could have become part of her 'expenses'. I would soon, however, have bored her. As long as I held a small piece of myself back from her, as long as I preserved a slight air of 'mystery', I had a chance of retaining my independence, and with it her interest and respect.

I certainly thought about making love to her, but I knew that I stood to lose much more than I would ever have gained from the momentary pleasure. Bette herself was a great believer in the saying that 'Sex is God's great joke on mankind', and I didn't want to make a laughing stock of myself in her eyes. Some friends have accused me of looking for a mother substitute in Bette but I had no need of a substitute. My relationship with my mother was perfect and Bette was certainly no competition in the maternal stakes. I loved Bette but I knew that I was handling dynamite. The slightest wrong move and I would be blown right out of her life.

We did discuss marriage at one stage, when I was applying to get my green card so that I could work in America. It was her contention that her previous four marriages had not worked out because none of the husbands were able to accept that they obviously would be 'Mr Bette Davis'. I had no such hang-up. I knew very well that I was never going to achieve anything close to what Bette has achieved in her life. I am quite secure enough to know that I could remain my own person and be married to a famous person. I would have been honoured to be 'Mr Davis', I would even have changed my name by deedpoll if she had asked and I know that I could have made her last years a great deal happier and healthier than they have turned out to be. I could have looked after her. In a situation like that, however, it was not for me to do the proposing. I was delighted when Bette suggested the idea.

We decided to think about it for a while, and I knew Bette would want to talk to B.D. about it. The next time I saw her she said that she had spoken to B.D., who did not want her mother to marry a man who was Jewish and half her age. Since B.D. married a man who was half-Jewish and twice her age, I'm not sure whether this was true or whether Bette was just looking for a reason to justify her own fear about getting into another marriage. I also doubt whether Bette would have let B.D.'s opinion stop her if she had really wanted to go ahead with the marriage.

If B.D. did have reservations about her mother marrying again, it is hardly surprising. She had lived through Bette's marriage to Gary Merrill and knew all too well how difficult Bette was to handle. She would have known that her mother was not cut out for marriage to anyone and may have grasped at whatever excuses she could think of. Also, naturally, no daughter wants her mother to marry again, particularly when she knows that there is no great love on her mother's side. Bette did not love me and B.D.'s decision, as told to me by Bette, was totally right and correct.

Living with Bette, it was not hard to see why she had so much trouble with her husbands. She really did like to bully and dominate everyone around her, and wouldn't have been able to tolerate any man strong enough to stand up to her. Yet that was exactly the sort of man she thought she wanted. Perhaps if, like Joan Crawford, she had married a really successful businessman, someone who was her equal but no competition, she might have made it.

There were times when I was with her when I felt tempted to hit her very hard – not something which I had been brought up to expect men to do to ladies. As her friend I was not in a position to do that. As her husband I would have been, and I suspect that the temptation would at times have been overwhelming, which would have immediately put our marriage in the same category as all her others. In a situation like that everyone castigates the man for using physical violence, but how else is he to protect himself if the woman attacks him? I suspect that Bette hit her husbands just as often as they hit her, and possibly a great deal harder. I also suspect she deserved everything she got from them.

Bette wrote that there were four major reasons why she believed marriages failed: money, having only one bathroom, an inability to communicate and sex. 'Nothing,' she said another time, 'not infidelity or boredom, can destroy love as quickly or completely as the physical abuse of one person by another.'

Her first marriage to Harmon Nelson was certainly a romantic love-match and Bette claimed she was still a virgin when they married. When she appeared on the Dick Cavett Show, Cavett asked her when she had first lost her virginity. Her quick reply to this impertinent question was: 'Would you believe it if I told you, when I got married?' – delivered as only Bette Davis could.

Harmon was a romantic, if rather weak, man and he lacked Bette's driving ambition. He was also unable to 'dominate' Bette, which was what she said she looked for in a man. In those days it was not done for a man to live off his wife's earnings, and before long Bette was earning ten times as much as her bandleader husband. They tried to boost his career by getting into radio and they even tried writing a popular song together, called 'Riding on a Bus Top', to launch him, but nothing worked. It meant that they had to live in a much smaller house than Bette could have afforded for herself, in order that 'Ham' could feel he was 'looking after' her. When Bette became pregnant there was no way she could afford to give up work and no way that Ham could support a family in the style Bette thought fit. The only answer was an abortion. This, she claimed, was the first of several.

They enjoyed their early days together in Hollywood, listening to music, going to movies and taking weekend trips down to San Diego where they would catch the ferry across to the famous Hotel del Coronado, which was later to act as a location for the Marilyn Monroe film *Some Like It Hot*, and where all of Hollywood seemed to go at the weekends. But there was a problem with their working hours. Bette was slaving in a hot studio all day and wanted a husband who would settle down and relax with her in the evenings. Ham, however, was just on his way out to work when she was getting in. As Bette became more famous Ham became more jealous and complaining.

Ham was still with her during the legal battle with Warners, which was fought in a British court, and they sailed over to England together. Things were not going well by then, however, and in the middle of the fight Ham announced that he was going back to America. Bette told me that it was one of the low points of her life, waving him off, knowing that she was all alone in England, struggling with a hostile legal establishment against the might of Jack Warner.

The marriage to Gary Merrill was also a romantic affair, and was more of a match of equals than the others. Merrill was never likely to be a star in the same league as his wife but he was a good actor with a decent career behind and ahead of him. It wasn't long, however, before his wife's outstanding success began to get him down. One film that was meant to be a vehicle for him, *Phone Call from a Stranger*, also had a small part for his wife. It shows how devoted Bette was that she agreed to take such a role for him, but it was a mistake. Even a small part in a film would turn it into a Bette Davis Movie, and Bette was able to upstage her husband all too easily.

In her book *My Mother's Keeper*, B.D. recounts some horrible scenes between her mother and step-father when she was a child. When she asked her mother why they couldn't leave Gary, Bette told her she was too young to understand, that all men were the same in the long run. She said all her husbands had beaten her up and that men liked to have power over their woman. They didn't like bright, strong women. However, after Bette, Gary romanced Rita Hayworth, so it must be concluded that he had not learned too much from his experiences with Bette!

Early on in our relationship Bette was going out with the head of one of the big paperback publishing houses. He was a remarkable man, very good-looking, charming, successful and rich. I would have thought he would have been an ideal candidate but she never explained to me what happened to him. Another time, when I hadn't seen her for a few months, she announced that she had a 'fiancé'. Both Vik and I decided that the last thing we needed in our lives was a 'fiancé', so we were determined to get rid of him before we had even met him. He worked on the production side of the Debbie Reynolds Show when Bette met him.

He flew over to England to stay with Bette and Vik, who went down to meet him at the airport and then rang me immediately.

'This is worse than we thought,' he told me. 'The man is a screaming queen. He's absolutely awful – and bald.'

Bette had organised a room for the fiancé at her hotel in Maidenhead, where Vik was also staying. In the middle of the night, Vik heard the window of his room sliding open. He snapped on the light to find Bette climbing in off the roof, in nothing but a mink coat.

'Oh, Vik!' she exclaimed, 'It's your room! I was just going to test out the "fiancé".'

Bette and I were planning to throw a four-day-long party at the country cottage belonging to my assistant's mother. Bette said she wanted this 'fiancé' to come. I pointed out that the house only had two bedrooms, but she said the 'fiancé' could stay in the caravan in the garden.

The party was for her birthday and for Easter. Guests who turned up during the four days included my mother and father, Roald Dahl and Patricia Neal, Sir Michael Redgrave, Sir Joseph Lockwood and Christian Roberts. At one stage Bette organised an Easter egg hunt in the house, using real eggs dyed different colours. She hid thirty of them in various places, making sure that one of them would never be found, to the consternation of our hostess who smelled it several weeks later.

Vik and I had decided that the best way forward was to allow the fiancé to hang himself. We just had to make sure that Bette got to see him in his true colours. I installed him in the caravan and when Bette arrived we sent her out to see him. The man was a total hypochondriac and the moment she saw his rows of pill bottles she could hardly bring herself to talk to him. Throughout the four days the poor man was begging everyone who arrived to give him a lift back to London and Bette was forbidding him to leave. She was very cruel to him. She spent most of the four days in the kitchen and at one stage she was laughing so much at the poor man's discomfiture that she allowed four of our hostess's precious crystal glasses to slide off the sink and break. The sound of them shattering had everyone in the sitting room jumping like cats on hot tin roofs. Of course she replaced the glasses, but she was unable to find any quite as fine as the ones she had destroyed.

When he finally made it back to Maidenhead the fiancé fled on the first transatlantic plane he could find, without even leaving a note. Bette rang me at home after the weekend. 'The bird has flown,' she said, chuckling. Looking back with hindsight, I wonder if Bette had her tongue in her cheek throughout the entire affair.

The shortage of rooms meant that the actor Christian Roberts and I had to share the one which led to the only bathroom in the cottage. Bette, who had a room on the other side of the staircase, arrived in our room just as I was swallowing a sleeping pill, announcing that she needed to use the bathroom. She proceeded to do just that and then emerged, with a face covered in cold cream and a scrabble board under her arm, and forced us to play the boardgame with her for an hour, perching herself, cross-legged, on the end of the bed. She really was so sweet and such fun then, but I couldn't enjoy this intimate time to its full as I kept dozing off.

Sometimes, late at night, when she was reminiscing, she would wonder whether she and 'Farney', her second husband would have made it if he hadn't died so young. Farney's death in Los Angeles had always been something of a mystery. Witnesses heard a terrible scream and saw him toppling over as he walked along Hollywood Boulevard, and making awkward movements. He was carrying a briefcase. His head hit the concrete pavement and he began to haemorrhage from his nose and ears. A crowd quickly formed around him as he lay, convulsing on the ground. During the disturbance it was later realised that the briefcase he had been carrying had disappeared.

Bette told me that when she was about three days into filming *Mr Skeffington*, a small boy arrived on the set and asked to see her. Thinking he was a fan they told him to go away and come back some other time but he insisted it was a matter of the utmost urgency. Bette agreed to come out to talk to him and saw he had Farney's briefcase. She invited the boy into her dressing room and he confessed that he had run off with the case when Farney fell. He opened it for her and showed her that it was full of liquor bottles. Bette had known that Farney was drinking heavily but not this heavily. She thanked the boy for returning the case and never mentioned the matter to anyone for many years.

She enjoyed telling the story of what happened to Farney's body. Apparently he came from a very wealthy New England family and his mother wanted the body brought back home, so Bette travelled back with it from Hollywood, even though she wanted to bury him out in California. She told B.D. that Farney was 'tied to his mother's apron strings. . . . and what a mother! Christ, what a cold bitch.'

The family had an estate and the mother had chosen a spot for the body but there was a granite formation round it, so there were bulldozers and teams of men with explosives trying to reach the exact spot. Everyone had to wait while the work was done before they could find Farney's final resting place. The trouble was that the mother kept changing her mind about where she wanted the final resting place to be.

Bette couldn't understand why she was unable to find success and happiness in her private life as she had in her professional world. She was very bitter about the way her marriage to Gary Merrill broke up. When he arrived at the house to collect their son Michael, she would shout at him to stay at the end of the drive and send Michael down to him. Knowing that, I was able to see what happened to people once Bette had decided that she didn't want them in her life any more. Like the pages of her Rollerdex, when you were out, you were most certainly out. I often wondered how long I had to go.

She always loved to hear about other people's romances and problems. She adored the Taylor/Burton saga, believing that it was good for her industry to have so much coverage in the press all the time. She would often act as a confidante to young actresses who were having trouble with their husbands and boyfriends. She invariably took the woman's side, believing that all men are basically the same 'bastards' as the ones she had been involved with over the years.

She often talked about her affair with Howard Hughes, claiming that she was the only woman who ever managed to bring the bisexual billionaire to a climax. He also won a place in her heart by making love to her on a bed covered with gardenias – her favourite flower. The affair with Hughes ended unpleasantly when her husband at the time, Harmon Nelson, bugged them together in Bette's house and threatened to send the tape to the press. In those days a story of adultery would have ruined Bette's career, and the situation was worsened when Hughes announced that he was going to sue Nelson for invasion of privacy. To dampen the whole thing down, Bette paid Hughes substantial damages herself, and he remained friendly with her, to the point of sending her flowers each year on the anniversary of the settlement.

At one time she had a much gossiped-about affair with Anatole Litvak, who directed her in *The Sisters*. He was a Russian who had made a name with his film of *Mayerling*. He was also married to Miriam Hopkins, one of Bette's greatest enemies.

At one stage Bette began to reminisce about the British actor, John Loder, whom she had admired in the early 1940s when he played supporting roles in a couple of her films, *Now Voyager!* and *Old Acquaintance*. Loder had gone on to marry Hedy Lamarr, with Bette becoming godmother to their daughter Denise, and they later divorced. Bette thought she would like to take up where she had left off.

'I would love to see Loder again,' she told me. So I secured a number for her and she rang him. They chatted for a while and then Loder began to realise what she was after.

'Bette,' he said, 'I think I must tell you that I am a very old man now. I am nearly eighty, I am bald and I think you would be very disappointed. I am not the man you remember from thirty years ago.'

To start with Bette didn't really take this in, but gradually it dawned on her that she had a picture in her mind of a man who no longer existed, and she politely drew the conversation to a close.

She had a similar experience with George Brent, who she actually hoped would ask to marry her during their affair. Twenty years later, while she was touring, George sent a bouquet of orchids backstage asking if he could come round to see her before the show. Bette quickly made herself up to receive her old admirer, and felt sad and a little cheated by the changed man who appeared.

Bette enjoyed telling stories of how jealous her husbands were of her. She told me that when her marriage to William Grant Sherry was collapsing, she found him very hard to shake off. His threats made her a virtual prisoner in the studio where she was working.

Sherry was a deceptively mild man, who had been disappointed in almost everything he had done. When Bette met him he was a 29-year-old artist living in Laguna; before that he had been an unsuccessful boxer. He was a moody, difficult man, fairly good-looking, lean, dark and hairy like all the men she was attracted to. At the time they were courting he was working as a male nurse. Bette met him at a party in Laguna Beach. He was just out of the Marines and America was still at War. Many ill-fated marriages were contracted at that time. Bette claimed that she had been romantically involved with another man, but that he had been sent off to Japan and she grew tired of waiting.

The family were horrified by Bette's choice and Bobby even hired a detective to investigate Sherry's past. After they were married Bette was told that Sherry had told his Marine colleagues in San Diego that his ambition when he left the Marines was to marry a wealthy woman. Sherry's mother was an elevator operator in San Diego, and Bette claimed to admire the way she had worked to support her two sons.

Marrying him was the worst thing Bette could have done, and they were frequently seen to be fighting in public. She often said that the only good thing to come out of it was B.D. By the time Bette became a mother she was thirty-nine years old. If she had waited any longer it would have been too late. It was a difficult birth by Caesarian section and B.D. was big – ten pounds ten ounces – even then. For a while the child held the marriage together. Bette was always intensely family conscious, and B.D. was the first new blood relative to enter her life since her mother and sister, and her sister's children. Bette took a year off work and B.D. became a Hollywood celebrity, visited in her cot by such questionable luminaries as Louella Parsons and Hedda Hopper. Bette, however, was clever enough to always make sure that she was on good terms with these powerful women of the press and, unlike other major stars, she never fell out with them.

For a while Bette lived the perfect family life that the fan magazines wrote about, making home movies, going to barbecues, and generally being a mother. When she started work again it looked as if she really would be able to balance the two worlds, but it wasn't to be long before she realised that marriage to Sherry was impossible. She moved into her dressing room at RKO Studios which was, in fact, a two-storey apartment with a bedroom, living room and make-up room. She tried one more reconciliation but finally left.

Bette claimed that Sherry got into a fight with her leading man at the time, Barry Sullivan, and then learned from her housekeeper that Sherry was having an affair with B.D.'s nurse, and they were planning to take the child away with them. A furious divorce and custody battle ensued, with Bette holding onto B.D. and sending Sherry packing. Sherry went on to marry the nurse, and now has children and grandchildren.

She always told me that William Wyler was the love of her life, and they certainly would have been evenly matched as far as talent and strength of personality were concerned. She claimed that after one particularly bitter row with him on the set of *The Little Foxes*, which they were making together, she stormed out. She subsequently received a letter with his handwriting on the envelope. She was so angry with him she left the letter, unopened, on the sideboard and didn't get round to reading it for a fortnight. When she did finally open it, she read that Wyler was asking her to marry him and saying that if he didn't hear from her within two weeks he was going to marry the young actress Margaret Talli-achet. She missed the deadline by hours and Wyler probably had the narrowest escape of his life.

It is generally believed that their affair started during the filming of *Jezebel*. Wyler's ability to make the most of her as an actress completely enthralled her. He had as fierce a drive as she, under a quiet exterior, and she was convinced that they could become a permanent partnership. They were both disciplined and severe in their approach to their work, dedicated to achieving the best. But Wyler found Bette's neuroses infuriating. She in turn enjoyed the idea of being dominated by a man, but at the same time wanted to dominate him.

Bette told me how when she first came to Hollywood she was directed in tests by Wyler, and he had been absolutely brutal to her. This was at Universal Studios. She saw that he would be a great director and, I believe, also admired him personally as well as professionally. She followed his career with keen interest and when she achieved stardom and was consulted on who should direct her, she wanted to have Wyler. Her opportunity came with *Jezebel*. Wyler was offered and accepted the film. He did not recog-nise the little girl from Universal but he was happy to have Bette Davis in the film. She never forgot that she was that same little girl.

In an interview with Photoplay she talked about the problems of the sex war:

Men continually work and fret themselves into bad tempers over their sex resentment of women's new-found independence in their careers, and what they don't know is the Great Fuss is in vain. Women never have, never will, never can be independent of the men they love – and be happy! All women know this. Only men are blind to it. And because it has made them so unhappy in general, this, to my mind, is the most important thing men do not know about themselves.

Men should boss women more! This is particularly true of American men. Women adore feeling they are possessed, that they belong to a dominant male. As I see it, the great danger in woman's new place in the scheme of things, is not nearly so menacing to women in that they will upset the applecart by wearing the pants – as it is that men are going to let them get away with it! All men need to do is quit pouting over their lack of dominance, and begin to assert it more. The women won't mind. They'll love it.

When she first started acting she met Henry Fonda, and fell for him. She actually managed to get out on a double date but, as Fonda was to recall when I talked to him much later, she was a 'plain little thing' and of no interest to him at all. She did succeed in kissing him, however, and this may well have been her first serious kiss. Fonda remembered:

When I met Bette she was a quiet little girl, then a few years later, at the Cape Playhouse, Dennis, Massachusetts we met again – I was third assistant stage manager and she was an apprentice, studying with the apprentice group at the playhouse and ushering.

Later that summer she got a break and played the ingenue part in something, and she blossomed. I would never have guessed at that time, that this little thing had the power that she has as an actress.

When you look at her films you see the range, the gamut, the A to Z she ran. I worked with her twice in films, and she won an Academy Award for *Jezebel* of course, the other was a pot boiler, didn't amount to very much, but it was a pleasant experience as far as working with Bette was concerned. We've always been good friends.

During the filming of *Jezebel*, Fonda had to leave the set for several days in order to be with his wife during the birth of their first child Jane. Bette agreed to play her scenes to a non-existent leading man while the next generation of Fondas got under way with the entrance of Jane into the world. Both father and daughter have always expressed great gratitude to Bette for this generous gesture.

Bette often ended up 'good friends' with the men she admired most. Spencer Tracy, for instance, was a man she claimed she would do anything for, but he was more interested in Katharine Hepburn. When Katharine Hepburn's biography was published, which dealt with Spencer's drink problems, Bette told me she contacted Katharine and offered her the services of her lawyer so that she could sue.

'I loved Spence before you did,' she told her, 'and you should sue.'

Hepburn curtly, and sensibly, refused the offer.

It is a strange irony that many of the sexiest people in the world are often the least interested in sex. Great talents, like the top people in Hollywood, tend to pour all their energies into their work, leaving very little for the bedroom. For most of them, however, the discipline needed to live the sort of professional lives that the big stars maintained leaves them very little private energy. Many lesser actors have had their professional lives ruined simply because they didn't have the self-discipline to say 'Not tonight.' For all her protestations to the contrary, I suspect that for most of her life Bette simply didn't have the time or energy for an active sex-life. If you insist on retiring to your bedroom at nine o'clock before every day's filming you are not going to get many opportunities to enjoy other energetic occupations.

I think she also enjoyed the bachelor life. When you live alone for a long time you get used to being able to stretch out across the bed, and to have as many pillows as you want. It would be hard for someone who had been on her own for so long to get used to sharing such a personal part of her life.

In *All About Eve*, Mankiewicz gave Bette these marvellous words about a career woman:

Funny business, a woman's career. The things you drop on your way up the ladder – so you can move faster – you forget you'll need them when you go back to being a woman. That's one career all females have in common whether we like it or not. Being a woman. Sooner or later, we've got to work at it, no matter what other careers we've had or wanted. And in the last analysis nothing is any good unless we can look up just before dinner – or turn around in bed – and there he is. Without that you're not a woman. You're someone with a French provincial office – or a book full of clippings. But you're not a woman.

Slow curtain. The end.

12

Monster

I loved Bette Davis but it would be foolish of me to deny that she was a bully. She was a powerful personality and she liked to exercise that power. She took arbitrary dislikes to people and was then merciless in her attacks on them. She also turned these attacks on the people who deserved them the least, and often on those who were least able to defend themselves.

The trouble usually started with drink. There has been a lot of speculation as to whether or not she was an alcoholic. I tend to think she was not, but she had a very low tolerance to alcohol. It went into her bloodstream quickly and after a while she became nasty. To begin with I used to try to tackle the problem by getting some food into her to soak up the alcohol. I soon discovered that this was the worst thing to do. It was when the food hit the drink that things really did start to get unpleasant. As she became older, particularly when she got back to the boredom of Hollywood, the cocktail hour became earlier and earlier, until she would sometimes start at four in the afternoon. I also believe that she was taking a couple of vodkas at lunchtime, although she never did while I was with her.

It was impossible to tell when she was going to turn unpleasant, or who would be the victim. Even Peggy Shannon, who was a devoted friend to her and couldn't have been less deserving of criticism, was sometimes the target. I still cringe at the thought of one dinner the three of us had in a London hotel. Bette seemed to be fine and offered Peggy some bread.

'Have some bread, Peggy!' She spat the name out with surprising venom.

'No thank you, Miss Davis,' Peggy said politely. It was a mistake to turn the bread down, but she had no cause to suspect what was coming.

'Bread is filthy, bread is disgusting, it's bad for you, but you love this particular bread, Peggy!' The eyes were widening, the mouth was turning down and I could sense danger approaching. 'I ordered it specially for you, Peggy!'

Peggy still wasn't sure what was happening, and politely declined any bread.

'This bread is for you, Peggy!' Bette snarled, standing up from the table, 'and you are going to eat it,' and she began to hit poor Peggy about the head with the miniature loaf.

Peggy burst into tears and left the table to compose herself. When she came back Bette was standing by the food trolley muttering to herself. She came over to Peggy, seemingly contrite. 'Peggy, darling,' she whined. 'Why are you crying? How could you ever believe that I would want to upset you? You are my dearest friend, I would never do anything to hurt you . . .', the lips curled down again . . . 'but you are going to eat the bread!'

The next day, as usual, she was contrite and horrified by what she had done. In recompense, she bought Peggy a beautiful silver cigarette case and had it engraved. But no matter how nicely she made up, we all knew that she could turn on us again at any time.

When things became unpleasant in hotels she would also start serving the food with her fingers rather than the utensils provided. She would hurl it onto your plate with her fingers as she served you – sausages, chops, whatever. It meant that she always seemed to have greasy fingers. Eating in public restaurants could also be embarrassing if Bette was not on form. When I first met her she liked going to Robert Carrier's restaurant in London, and on one occasion other diners started to complain because the noise coming from our table was so obnoxious. Although Mr Carrier was very charming and said he had been delighted to meet Bette, I could tell that he was not very impressed by her behaviour.

Sometimes, when she went out without me, I would receive a phone call the next morning. 'Well,' she would announce, 'I smashed up another damn dinner party.' She seemed almost proud of the fact that she 'could louse up a dinner party quicker than anyone'.

Roald Dahl actually asked her to leave his house during one dinner party where she started to insult another guest, who was an English professor. Pat Neal Dahl had set out a lovely table covered by a beautiful cloth and the professor upset a glass of wine on it. He was most apologetic, but Bette went on about the bloody

English who thought Americans were so rich that they wouldn't care if you ruined their table cloths. Roald wasn't one to put up with anything from anyone, even Bette Davis, and so he asked her to leave.

It was as if she had to have some sort of turbulence in her life. Whenever things were going too smoothly or pleasantly she would have to berate somebody. She liked to demonstrate that she could dominate anyone, man or woman, but she only ever behaved badly when she had an audience. If you were alone with her, one to one, she was always delightful. You could discuss subjects and argue with her in the normal way, and she would treat you just as respectfully as you treated her. As soon as there were three or more people, however, she started to perform and to prove what a 'fighter' she was.

On every movie she made she had to have someone to hate. It could be someone as innocent as an assistant director whose voice was too loud, but it would give her an opportunity to rant and rave after shooting in the evening: 'Will nobody rid me of this man?' Every time the poor man shouted for the actors she would yell back, 'Don't shout! We are not cattle!'

She knew of her reputation for being a tyrant, and she was actually proud of it. 'Anyone can be liked,' she would tell me, 'but it takes guts to be a monster!'

She only turned on me twice in our friendship, and both times I managed to weather the storm. The first time was when I had not known her for long and I had arranged for a couple of producers to come to the house to meet her. I was young and new in the business and this was an important break for me. These men were impressed that I was able to set up a meeting with Bette Davis and I was feeling pretty proud of myself.

At that time I didn't know all of Bette's little habits and I offered to refill the producers' cocktail glasses. As I went to the bar, Bette swept up, hit my arm with all her strength and announced loudly, 'I pour the drinks in my house.' I was mortified at this humiliation and the two men were embarrassed to have to witness it. I said nothing, however, and Bette must have realised how unkind she had been to her young admirer because when their glasses were all empty again she looked up at me through her eyelashes.

'Roy, darling,' she said girlishly, 'will you freshen up our drinks? After all, this is your party.'

The second time was altogether more unpleasant. I was looking after Anne Francis at the time, another strong Hollywood actress, when Bette demanded that I should come to dinner. I told her I was with Anne, so she said, 'Bring her along', as she always did when I had a date on an evening when she wanted my company. I wasn't too sure but Anne, who was a good friend of Barbara Stanwyck's, said she would be delighted to meet Bette.

It was a long way out to Ascot from Anne's hotel and we were a little late setting out, so by the time we got to the house Bette had had a few drinks. Things started to go wrong when she began attacking New York, saying it was a filthy, disgusting place. Anne Francis very politely insisted that she couldn't agree. She had been brought up and lived in New York and she loved it.

Bette then turned her attention to me, and became violently anti-British. We were all dirty, stupid and everything else she could think of. At the time I was missing a tooth and waiting to have a replacement made, as was the director of the picture she was making, whom she loathed. This infuriated her and she rounded on me, saying that this was a typical example of our disgusting habits – we could not even take care of our teeth. I rode the storm out quietly and when we went through to the lounge she started to pour coffee.

'How do you like it, Roy?' she asked.

'Bette, you've known me long enough to know how I take my coffee!' I said quietly.

She finished pouring for us and then stood up, came over to me and put on her most irritating Baby Jane voice, her face twisted, ugly and little girlish.

'I think I've been a naughty girl,' she lisped. 'I think I'd better go to bed,' and with that she departed meekly upstairs.

On the way home I apologised profusely to Anne, who was very gracious about it. After a few moments' thought, however, she added, 'But Barbara Stanwyck is a nicer person.'

Bette was also very bad at dealing with the sort of sycophancy which surrounds all big stars. I once had a dinner engagement with a theatrical agent, who was completely in awe of Bette. She insisted that we both join her for dinner at her hotel. Once we were there she decided that she would like the duck, but it was only served for two people. I had already decided what I wanted, and it certainly was not duck, whether Bette fancied it or not. The agent said that he would share duck with her, which was fine, but then he had to add, 'And then I can say that I shared duck with Bette Davis.' Her temper began to boil then, and by the middle of the meal she exploded and stormed off to her room. I followed her upstairs and managed to calm her down, even talking her into writing an apology to the man, but I could see her point. Sycophancy is one of the most unattractive sides of human nature, and is something which film stars have to put up with all too often.

When Bette took a dislike to someone she would simply say, 'I'm gonna kill 'em,' and you knew that, with very few exceptions, she was going to destroy the object of her venom, certainly for the duration of that dinner party or evening. She had two terms of abuse which applied to anyone who displeased her: they were 'yella bellies' and they talked 'herse shit!' She could also keep a vendetta boiling for ages, particularly during the making of a film. Olivia de Havilland tells a terrible story of the first time she worked with Bette.

It happened while Olivia was still filming *Gone With The Wind*, and she had been cast to play in *Elizabeth and Essex* with Bette Davis and Errol Flynn. She had made Jack Warner promise her that she didn't have to do anything on his film until she had finished *Gone With The Wind* – not even a costume fitting or a discussion. When she had a morning off, however, she went to the set of *Elizabeth and Essex* to see what was happening and to watch Bette at work. When she got there Bette was rehearsing to herself in a corner and everything was quiet when an unfortunate call boy came up to Olivia and said, 'Miss de Havilland, how nice to see you. I can give you your call for tomorrow morning.'

Olivia said, 'No, no, you are wrong, I'm still on *Gone With The Wind*.'

The call boy insisted that she was on his list and, stupidly, she panicked and had a very loud and high-pitched row with the boy there and then. The set came to a standstill. Bette stopped rehearsing and 'popped' her eyes at the cause of this disturbance, watching the pretty young actress who was working on *Gone with the Wind*, the one film she had wanted to be part of. Olivia was led crying from the set and was not called until the following week, as had been agreed.

When she did report for duty nobody said a word to her. When Bette arrived on the set she made a point of kissing absolutely everyone from the director to the call boy, except Olivia de Havilland. She did the same thing every morning from then on, leaving Olivia in Coventry for her one outburst of temper.

A few years later Olivia was asked to co-star opposite Bette in *In This Our Life*, which was directed by John Huston. This time Olivia was determined not to take any nonsense, but on the first day Bette went up to her and said, 'You are one hell of an actress.' They played sisters, one bad one called Stanley, played by Bette of course, and one good called Roy and played by Olivia. It was an unusual film which sadly failed although it followed Huston's brilliant *The Maltese Falcon*. The two actresses became firm friends for the duration of the film. Olivia fell hopelessly in love with John Huston, who didn't return the feelings. Bette told me how Olivia used to spend hours in the bath with Bette scrubbing her back and listening to her tales of woe. Bette loved administering to people with broken hearts. Their friendship continued, precariously, for many years.

When Bette was a young actress on Broadway there was a big star named Laura Hope Crews. This grande dame was extremely unpleasant to Bette and eventually smacked her on the face. Many years later Bette was given the script for *The Man Who Came to Dinner*, and she saw the name Laura Hope Crews on the schedule for the following two days. Her hatred was still burning bright after all those years and overnight she worked herself up into a frenzy of venom, ready to take on this gorgon now that she, Bette, was the queen and Laura had been reduced to being a small part player.

The next day Bette came on set and Laura was there, a sick, old woman. Bette suffered an immediate change of heart and walked over to her and said: 'Miss Crews, I welcome you to this set, and look forward to playing our scenes together.' Laura, who never realised this was the same girl that she had treated so badly all those years ago, was completely taken aback and at the end of the second day's shooting she gave Bette a magnificent jewelled watch, which had been handed down to her from other actors. She pressed it into Bette's hand, saying, 'I want you to have this Miss Davis,' and disappeared. She died two weeks later, and her scene was cut from the film. Perhaps Bette had seen a horrible little flash of her own future.

Her enmities would often start when she had to compete with other actresses for parts, particularly in the old days of the studios. One such hatred developed between her and Miriam Hopkins and lasted to the grave. It started when Bette won the lead in *Jezebel*, which Miss Hopkins thought belonged to her. It developed when Miss Hopkins became convinced that Bette was having an affair with her husband, Anatole Litvak. Although Bette almost certainly went on to have an affair with Litvak, she was still in love with William Wyler when Miss Hopkins thought the affair was happening.

Miss Hopkins was an intelligent and ruthless Southern Belle, with unusual good looks, pretty but not beautiful. She became obsessively jealous of Bette. They made *The Old Maid* together and fought incessantly. Miss Hopkins actually managed to make herself more unpopular than Bette with her tantrums, and if Bette had been cleverer she would have learned a lesson from Miss Hopkins, seeing just how people disliked working with a 'monster'. Miss Hopkins was a very big star with much talent which Bette admired, but she also earned Bette's eternal dislike. Later, when I heard that she had died I passed the news on to Bette and her response was unequivocal.

'God has been good to us,' she replied. 'He's taken Miriam.'

Because of her reputation for being a tyrant, some producers and directors tried to get their way by stealth, and got themselves into even deeper trouble. In *Connecting Rooms* the producer wanted Alexis Kanner, a young Canadian television actor, to play the part of the young man in this rather bad script. I was meeting Bette at the airport that day, and I noticed all these people lurking furtively around. As she came through I was pushed aside by the eager production people, and Bette was whisked out to a car and taken to the hotel which I had arranged for her. I was angry and decided to drive back into London. I was going to a very important show that evening and so decided to take it easy back at home. Soon after I arrived back the 'phone rang and it was Bette calling from the hotel.

'Where are you?' she asked. 'Why aren't you here?'

'You saw what happened at the airport,' I explained. 'You seemed to be busy.'

'It was nothing to do with me,' she protested. 'I don't treat my friends like that. Come down to the hotel now.'

They asked her to see the young actor immediately, even though she had spent the last three days travelling, and she decided in her exhausted state that he was all right for the part. He was a charming young man, but he certainly wasn't right for this character.

She said, 'He looks good, and at least he's a man.'

'You're wrong,' I said, but she had made up her mind. I knew she was going to live to regret the decision, but there was nothing I could do. I thought that another actor, called Keith Baxter, should have been considered for the part, although he protested that he was too old for it.

At the end of the first week's filming she called me and was close to tears, which was very unusual.

'It's no good,' she said, 'we can't have this boy. You're absolutely right. Get Keith Baxter down here now.'

This was three o'clock on a Sunday afternoon, but I managed to get Keith there by five o'clock. They talked and loved each other on sight. She did everything she could to get him in, but the producer said that they now had too much of Alexis in the can. Bette became so desperate about getting Alexis Kanner up to scratch that she let him and the director work in her caravan between shots, while she paced around Pinewood, smoking and rehearsing herself.

One day when I went down, the director was not on the set, having gone home feeling unwell. During the filming Bette had also managed to work up a deep hatred for fellow actress Kay Walsh, and the feeling was mutual. After the director had gone Bette said:

'Cast and crew gather round me. We don't want to let him down. We all know what he wanted us to do today, so why don't we do it? And also today is Miss Walsh's last day.'

Bette made sure that the last scene she had to play with Miss Walsh was completed, then, as she prepared to leave the set, Bette threw her arms around her in a tight embrace and told her how happy she had been to work with such a fine actress – which Miss Walsh undoubtedly is. I caught a glimpse of her face over Bette's shoulder and it was a sight to behold!

But when Bette was working with Sir Michael Redgrave it was

like magic. At the end of some of the shots the whole unit would actually applaud them. But other parts of the production continued to push her patience to the limit. She disliked working on location anyway, and one sequence was being shot in Bayswater. Bette had been given a squalid little hotel room as a dressing room. When she came outside to film, a woman in the crowd started shouting abuse at the whole crew for filming in her square, disrupting her life. Something snapped inside Bette and she returned the lady's abuse in no uncertain manner, in front of the whole crowd, and stormed back into the ghastly little room. A few minutes later she managed to regain her self-control and came out to make a little speech of apology for her language to the crowd of over two hundred people.

Sometimes she deliberately laid into someone, in order to ensure that they stayed alert. Early on in the filming of *The Anniversary*, Christian Roberts had to stand on a particular mark just next to Bette in order to place a coffee table on which she would put her glass in the frame. The mark was very faint, and he missed it. The director was understanding and simply asked him to do it again, but Bette was angry.

'For goodness sake! Why don't you do it right?' she snarled, and Christian was so taken aback that he has never missed another mark or a single line throughout his career since. However, Christian is the first person to agree that although he felt humiliated at the time, he was being taught by the best.

Most of our bumpy nights, however, were of the sort I have described with Peggy Shannon, or with members of her family. I soon learned that the only way to deal with them was to keep quiet and ride them out. To fight with her would only enrage her still further, as probably happened in her marriages, until she either attacked physically or else broke the friendship off forever. In the morning the moods would nearly always have passed. In some cases the objects of her attacks were thoroughly deserving of everything they got.

Often the problem was that she simply saw matters out of proportion and flew off into a rage before she had time to think. B.D. once nearly hit a stray dog in her car. She swerved to miss it and crashed the car, breaking her arm and leaving her son Ashley badly shaken. Bette was furious and wanted to start a campaign against people who allowed their dogs to stray onto roadways. She yelled and shouted and, as often happens, soon turned the drama round so that it was 'poor Bette' rather than poor B.D. and poor Ashley. 'My daugher and grandson could have been killed by that dog!'

13

Bette and Other Stars

Despite the fact that she was the Queen of Hollywood, Bette always remained a devoted admirer of many of the big names who came before her, and she was never slow in handing out praise – or even writing fan letters – to young talents whom she admired. She seldom went to the theatre or the movies, because of the distraction she tended to cause. If she was in a theatre and the audience realised she was there, they would all be turning and craning their necks to get a glimpse of her, which she didn't think was fair to the performers on stage.

Christian Roberts and I once visited her at the Plaza Hotel in New York. When we went down to dinner there was a card on the table advertising the Persian Room, a cabaret room at the hotel in which many of the top stars have appeared. I idly picked up the card while we waited to order.

'Look, Bette,' I said, 'Rosalyn Kind is playing here.'

'So what?'

'She's Barbra Streisand's half-sister. I would really love to see her.'

Bette, who also admired Streisand, agreed that it would be interesting and called over the head waiter. She told him that we would like to be taken to the Persian Room after the house lights had gone down, and asked him to prepare a table for us at the back, so that we could pop in and out without anyone noticing. The arrangements went like clockwork. We went through back corridors and were ushered, in the dark, to our table. Rosalyn Kind appeared and performed for about twenty minutes, and then she stopped abruptly.

'Ladies and gentlemen,' she announced, 'I can't go on any further without telling you that in this room tonight is the greatest actress in the world.'

'Oh nuts!' growled the greatest actress in the world – but only we could hear.

The spotlight found her and she was very gracious about it but throughout the rest of the show the waiters were sent over in a steady stream by the other members of the audience with menus and requests for signatures.

There was a small movie house in Westport which she sometimes visited, where she could sit in a separate glass viewing room in front of the projection booth with a few friends. When *Love Story* came out she expressed a desire to see it, having admired the book. We went for a Chinese meal opposite the cinema first, and by the time we got to the cinema there was an enormous line for the next performance, even though the last one was still going on. It was freezing cold in the middle of a typical New England winter. Bette didn't want to hang around in the foyer on display until our friends arrived, so she went on up to the viewing room, happy to see the end of the film before the rest of us came in. By the time we got up to join her she was coughing and in floods of tears. The tiny room was filled with cigarette smoke. The ending of the film had left her distraught and she was loving every moment of it.

The next day she wrote a fan letter to Ryan O'Neal, in such a hurry that she didn't even spell his name correctly. I can imagine what a kick it must have given the young actor to receive a fan letter from the first lady of his industry. Later he showed his appreciation of her talents on one of the awards shows by kneeling at her feet and kissing her hand.

If I asked Bette who she admired most amongst actresses, she always mentioned Garbo with reverence. I offered to try to set up a meeting for her with her heroine if she wanted. At first she was keen but later she backed out, afraid that Miss Garbo would think she was pestering her. I tried to explain that Garbo would probably be as interested to meet Bette Davis as the other way round.

She explained to me that in the old days of Hollywood the stars of one studio seldom got to meet those of other studios, unless they led very hectic social lives which she had never had the time to do. Mae West was another of the legends whom she very much wanted to meet, and it was arranged for Bette to go up to her apartment. Miss West did not approve of drinking or smoking, but an ashtray was negotiated for Bette and they talked for a while.

Bette was fascinated. Everything in Miss West's apartment was pure white and gold, with satin-covered furniture. A butler hovered in the next room throughout the interview, out of sight but on hand should Miss West need him. Bette was dying to see if there were mirrors on the ceiling of her bedroom, as Hollywood legend had it, but didn't pluck up the courage to sneak a look. The elderly Miss West still wore twelve-inch heels on her shoes and very soon asked if Bette had a lover. Bette told her that she hadn't had one for many years, and Miss West advised her to remedy the situation.

Miss West always liked to give visitors little presents, and she offered Bette a choice between some earrings and a necklace or a belt. Bette chose the belt and afterwards told me that she wished she had taken the jewellery. I knew all about Miss West's presents and I said that since they all came from Woolworths or the likes, I didn't think it mattered what she took. Bette later returned Miss West's hospitality, inviting her to dinner at the house in Orlando with the famous opera singer Beverley Sills also present.

Bette admired Lana Turner greatly, and said that she particularly liked her performance in *Cass Timberlane*, opposite Spencer Tracy. Susan Hayward had also produced a couple of performances which Bette said she would have been proud to have given – which was the highest praise she could possibly heap on someone else's work. She also admired Rita Hayworth – the princess of Hollywood, where Bette was the queen – but felt somewhat piqued about Rita's long romance with Gary Merrill after his divorce from Bette.

Out of the British film industry, she was a great admirer of Celia Johnson, believing that the way Miss Johnson delivered The Speech for her departing husband in Noël Coward's *In Which We Serve*, had to make her a great actress. While she was in England on a visit she managed to get an invitation to Miss Johnson's house for lunch. There was nothing Bette liked better than to be invited to other people's houses. She loved to just wander around them, drinking it all in. Miss Johnson, however, was not playing that game. I don't know exactly what went wrong. I do know that they had lunch on the terrace and that when Bette realised she wasn't going to be invited inside the house she asked for the toilet, only to be pointed to an outside door. I also know that she came back in a disappointed mood, saying that Celia Johnson was something of a cold fish.

She always thought Laurence Olivier was wonderful. One hot

111

summer's day in Hollywood, a great moment occurred. I was at home at the Magic Hotel, lying on the floor, when Olivier phoned me on my private, outside line because he was in great distress over what was happening to his film *The Jazz Singer*. He was using me to confide in. We were having a very long talk when the other 'phone, which went through the hotel switchboard, also rang. It was Bette.

'Who the hell are you talking to?' she demanded. 'Your line has been busy for hours.'

'Laurence Olivier,' I told her.

She stopped in her tracks. 'Okay. Call me when you've finished. I'll take second billing to him anytime.'

'No hang on, Bette,' I said. 'I know he'd love to speak to you.' So I stretched out both telephones so that they were touching, and said: 'Laurence Olivier, this is Bette Davis, Bette Davis, this is Laurence Olivier.'

She may have loved Laurence Olivier but she did not like Vivien Leigh. This I believe was partly due to Vivien taking *Gone With The Wind* and *Streetcar Named Desire* from her, but also because Vivien played a trick on her in England, or at least so Bette believed. The Oliviers had invited her and her husband Gary Merrill down to their country house, but Vivien neglected to tell Bette that they dressed for dinner. Bette consequently came downstairs in slacks, to find everyone else decked out in full, formal finery. She always believed that Vivien had deliberately set her up for that.

Vivien was once asked to take over the role opposite Bette in *Hush Hush Sweet Charlotte*, when Joan Crawford dropped out of the film at the last minute. She later told me that she asked them for so much money she knew they wouldn't give it to her. 'I could just stand the thought of facing Joan Crawford at seven in the morning,' she told me, 'but I couldn't stand the thought of facing Bette Davis at that hour.'

Towards the end of Vivien's life I visited her and told her how kind Bette had been to me, and she asked me for Bette's address. Later, when Vivien had passed on, Bette went into an obscene tirade against her. I discovered that Vivien had sent her a postcard but had only signed her first name. The postcard was very pleasant, but Bette had no idea who it was from and threw it on the fire. When I told her that Vivien had asked me for her address she realised what had happened, and for once she seemed shamed into silence.

Had Vivien not died so tragically young, I doubt if I would ever have been able to get to know Bette so well. They were my two greatest actress friends, but had I continued to be as close to Vivien as I had been, I doubt if Bette would have allowed me to become quite such a close friend of hers. Vivien and Bette are the only two actresses whom I have known really well. I did not get to know Vivien as intimately as Bette, because I was not able to know her for as long but I have to say that I liked her more, both for her beauty and her wisdom.

Although we couldn't go to many public places of entertainment, Bette and I watched a lot of television together. It was an unnerving and overwhelming experience for me the first time I sat through one of her films with the real Bette Davis sitting right next to me. Over the years I became used to dissociating the woman next to me from the woman on the screen, partly because Bette was always so calm about it. She seldom seemed moved by her own performances. She generally watched them in silence and at the end would say something like, 'I wasn't too bad in that.' Most of the things we watched together were old movies, although she loved some of the soap operas and educated me on the intricacies of the plots.

There was one particular newscaster Bette had taken a fancy to and she talked to him on the screen as if he was in the room with her. 'How are you today, Jimmy?' she would ask. 'You are looking a little peeky; I think you should be taking better care of yourself.'

She was also a great fan of Glenda Jackson. When Miss Jackson won the Oscar for *Women In Love* she was not present at the Awards ceremony so Bette rang her up at 4.30 in the morning, British time, to break the news – and she hadn't even met her. 'Glenda Jackson,' she explained to me, 'is me today.'

Bette was also a fan of certain politicians. Nobody in the Kennedy or Roosevelt families could do any wrong in her eyes, and President Sadat was also a great hero of hers. At the time of the Israeli/Egypt peace agreement she visited Jimmy Carter at the White House, and she was told that Sadat was in the Oval Office with Carter.

'More than anything in my life I wanted to meet the man,' Bette

113

told me later, 'and I knew he was just in that room, but I couldn't get to him for all the secret service people.

'I became friendly with the police on duty outside the Oval Office, and asked if I could stand with them as he left. As the President of Egypt approached, President Carter introduced us and I threw my arms around Sadat's neck and kissed him, and told him I thought he was the most wonderful man in the world and that I had always admired him.'

She took a similarly forthright approach when she was at dinner with Lyndon B. Johnson. She managed to acquire two photographs of him and went up to the top table. She leaned over and said to the President:

'Excuse me, Mr President, please may I have your autograph. I'm Bette Davis. I would like one for myself and one for my son Michael Merrill.'

Needless to say he obliged, although Bette told me she doubted if he knew who she was.

During the Second World War the West Coast of America became a centre for the boys being sent out to fight in the Pacific. Los Angeles was the last soil that they would stand on before facing their ferocious enemies and many of them wanted to see the stars in Hollywood. I was once privileged to spend a day with Prince Charles when he was passing through California and had been invited to visit Universal Studios. One of the reporters in the party asked him why, when he was only spending one day in the area, he had asked to come to a film studio. 'Where else do you go on your first day in Hollywood?' he asked. The young soldiers and sailors felt the same, but of course few were getting the opportunity to see their idols.

John Garfield, a great Warner Bros star at the time, had the idea of starting a 'Hollywood Canteen' for the troops, with stars serving and entertaining them. He needed someone to run it and he invited Bette to lunch with him at the Green Room at Warners (which was actually blue), and invited her to be the chairperson. She was delighted and set about the job with a vengeance. They found a building a block away from Sunset Boulevard which had previously been a theatre and a succession of nightclubs, and leased it for $100 a month. The building was in a terrible state, but they managed to persuade studio craftsmen to set it right, and cartoonists provided murals for the walls. They then set about raising money with supper dances and other events. They were so successful at fund-raising that by the time the war was over the Canteen had half a million dollars in the bank, which Bette helped to distribute around various charities. While it was up and running they averaged two shifts of three thousand men each night. There were over three and a half thousand volunteer dance hostesses registered with the Canteen, and artists putting on shows at little notice.

According to Bette the Canteen employed a paid staff of nine and had six thousand volunteer workers to call on. Each night they needed a crew of one hundred as well as the hostesses to sweep up and set out the tables, to make the sandwiches, wash dishes, run the cloakrooms and man the doors through midnight. Bette's main task was to round up stars and work out the rosters. She told me that it was surprising how many of them told her they had 'early calls' the next day and had to get to bed on time! She thought that a most ungenerous attitude. Warners later made a film called *Hollywood Canteen*, and Bette said that more stars appeared in that than had shown up for the real thing. Some of them, however, were always helpful. Betty Grable never let her down and, according to Bette, actually met and married band-leader Harry James at the Canteen. Marlene Dietrich could also be relied on. One evening Marlene, who was filming *Kismet* during the day, arrived straight from the set covered from head to toe in gold paint. The troops loved it. Hedy Lamarr and Dorothy Lamour also helped out a great deal.

One Christmas Eve, Bette was let down by a star who had promised to come and entertain. She was desperate, and rang Bing Crosby.

'What do you want me to do?' Bing asked.

'I don't know,' Bette replied, 'anything. Just come down.'

A little while later Bing turned up with his four sons and they gave an impromptu concert, including, of course, 'White Christmas'. Bette told me that for her that was one of the high spots of the whole Canteen project.

'I did a lot of "calling",' she told me, 'and the Victory Committee – after the Canteen had started – tried to stop us. They said we couldn't call people up personally. I said, "We have fifteen guilds and unions in this Canteen, and if we don't call people up personally, if we have to go through your Victory Committee, our

Canteen's finished." I told them that if they didn't allow me to continue contacting people personally I would have to close the Canteen, advise the guilds and unions who had been part of the formation team and send a statement to the press. At six the next morning they rang to tell me I could continue doing it the personal way. A lot of people worked out in the kitchens. Mrs John Ford was there all the time for three and a half years. Some of the stars (who shall be nameless) wouldn't do the kitchen, because they wanted to be out front. I never did the kitchens, because I had to be in the front, as a celebrity, and sign autographs and do my stuff.'

It has to be said in fairness that all the stars should have been, and mostly were, out front. They were the people whom the troops had come to see.

'It was a big job, and I must say for Mr Warner that I was on the 'phone all day long – people would call me – and he never beefed.'

Bette found getting to know the boys, knowing that they were being shipped out to almost certain death, was heart-breaking. She told me that she found out where the secret harbour was that they were sailing from, and she used to stand in the hills and watch the ships leave port, just waving, crying and hoping that she had been able to do something to brighten their last few days ashore. Having said that, she never actually went out to entertain the troops as many of the other stars did. Perhaps she was too busy filming, but she did travel round the country on bond drives. Her contribution to the war effort was appreciated by President Roosevelt who invited her to his private residence, which was an enormous thrill for such a staunch Democrat.

When she first arrived in Hollywood she was particularly fond of Jean Harlow who, although younger than Bette, was already a star. In the early stages Bette did not, as Katharine Hepburn and Margaret Sullavan did, manage to stop the studios from trying to change her into a starlet. The first time the make-up people and hairdressers got to work on her they tried to turn her out as an imitation Harlow. It was not a success and she was soon able to impress her own personality onto her work – and her looks.

When Jean Harlow's husband later committed suicide, Bette proved to be an invaluable friend to the star, as she often was to

116

The National Film Theatre, London

Right: On stage.

Below: Afterwards, checking whether it shows that one of Bette's 'lifts' has gone.

At the cottage in Buckinghamshire

Above: Bette and me with an unexpected guest (behind) and Christian Roberts (right).

Left: Bette visiting the 'fiancé's' caravan.

Left and below: Alone at last after the 'fiancé's' departure.

Bette with my Mini.

Left: With Sir Joseph Lockwood, then Chairman of EMI.

Below: With Patricia Neal, Roald Dahl's wife. *(Photo by Arnold Weissberger.)*

Some of Bette's favourite paintings

Bette as Margot Channing in *All about Eve*, painted by an admirer.

Bette as Jezebel.

B.D.

Bette and Me

A very happy Christmas evening with my mother and father at the
Grosvenor House Hotel.

The 70th Birthday Party

A 'blacked up' Bette welcomed all her personal guests to a private party in her apartment in Hollywood.

people when they were in genuine distress. Bette enjoyed all Harlow's films, as well as liking her as a person.

She also liked Marion Davies, the young actress who was the mistress of William Randolph Hearst, the newspaper magnate. This led to her being invited to some of the famous Hearst parties at San Simeon, the fabulous castle Mr Hearst built for himself at Big Sur. Orson Welles' *Citizen Kane* was based, none too loosely, on Mr Hearst. San Simeon typified the sort of outrageous glamour which the general public believed life was like every day in Hollywood. Hearst literally bought a mountain overlooking the coast and hauled a castle to the top of it. Gold-leafed, Olympic-sized swimming pools, guest suites the size of villas and dining halls fit for Henry VIII, all created an ambience which meant few people could resist accepting invitations. Full-sized palm trees were sailed into the harbour below, and pulled to the top of the mountain, to form the basis for the exotic gardens which were laid out on the bare, mountain soil. Hearst imported herds of wild animals from Africa, and allowed them to roam over the mountainside in his private zoo.

These days San Simeon is run by the state of California as a popular tourist attraction. The house is so large that there are two separate half-day tours which cover different parts of the house. It is a fabulous palace, built to honour the great conquerors of early Hollywood, who marched across the screen of the world and brought back their riches to the West Coast of America.

Later, it was in this sort of illustrious company that Bette discovered the joys of La Costa, a health resort in the California desert near San Diego, where she would continue to disappear to all her life when she felt in need of 'rejuvenation', to enjoy massages and to lie around palm-fringed pools.

Amongst the following generation of actresses Bette admired Debbie Reynolds, who had a small part in *June Bride* and later co-starred with Bette in *A Catered Affair*. She befriended the young Ann Margret, who was the only person she liked while making *Pocketful of Miracles*, and followed her career with interest from then on. She was impressed by the young Kathryn Grant who was dating Bing Crosby when Bette met her. Kathryn confided that she intended to marry Bing and proceeded to do so. Bette admired that sort of guts and determination. She also liked Bing Crosby – one of the few people who did – and disliked Bob Hope immensely.

When working on *June Bride*, Bette met another young actress called Betty Lynn, who was to remain a good friend to her for over forty years.

In *All About Eve*, she appeared with Marilyn Monroe and always spoke highly of her professionalism. Bette also liked her co-star in *All About Eve*, Anne Baxter, immensely. Anne later went on to play the part of Margot Channing in *Applause*, a musical version of the film which was produced on Broadway. She asked Bette to come and see her and Bette agreed to sit in the wings. She thought Anne was excellent, much better than her predecessor Lauren Bacall.

Lauren Bacall had actually been brought to meet Bette when she was a teenage usherette in New York. She had somehow become friendly with Robin Brown, Bette's old acting-school friend, and they visited Bette for tea at the Dakota House, where Bette was staying at the time. Lauren recalls the incident in her biography but according to Bette she leaves out one telling scene.

'What Miss Bacall leaves out,' Bette was to say, 'was that as she left she fell into a dead faint, and had to be carried back into the apartment again.'

Lauren went on to express gratitude to Bette for her kindness to her when she, Lauren, was given her big break in Hollywood at the age of nineteen opposite Humphrey Bogart in *To Have and Have Not*, making possibly the most auspicious debut in films. Lauren went on to marry Bogart – whom Bette did not like, believing him to be pompous and uninteresting.

In common with others, Bette disliked Glenn Ford intensely. While making *Pocketful of Miracles*, Ford gave an interview in which he said that out of gratitude to Bette for casting him in her production of *A Stolen Life*, he had insisted she play in *Pocketful of Miracles* in order to rescue her from obscurity. Bette was beside herself with fury. Of course this story is utter nonsense. Frank Capra was the director and it was he who would have decided who to cast. It was the first time the great director had had the opportunity to work with Bette Davis. They did not like each other once the film was finally completed, although Bette was to pay tribute in person to Capra many years later when he was honoured, as she had been, by the American Film Institute.

She did not like Leslie Howard, whom she found cold and uninteresting. She knew that when they were casting *Human Bondage* Howard had not wanted her for the part of Mildred, since he considered that she was not experienced enough. When they worked together later on *The Petrified Forest*, she told the press that she adored him, when in fact they barely exchanged a word on the set.

She thought Robert Montgomery, who she starred opposite in *June Bride*, was 'overbearing, pompous and ridiculously right wing', and never warmed to Monty Woolley who came out from Broadway to recreate his great success as Sheridan Whiteside in *The Man Who Came to Dinner* when she had wanted the dying John Barrymore to play the part.

Mary Astor and Bette had a great mutual respect for one another. In *The Great Lie*, Mary Astor won an Oscar for best supporting actress and sent Bette a cable: 'Thank you for my Oscar – Astor.'

Bette admired Ann Sheridan as 'a no-nonsense dame', and enjoyed working with Gladys Cooper. She did not like Ginger Rogers, Ingrid Bergman, Barbara Stanwyck or Joan Collins. She loved Elizabeth Taylor, despite the fact she lost *Virginia Woolf* to her.

At the time of making *All About Eve* she did not like Celeste Holm, who played the cool, writer's wife. However, Bette often said that the scene in the car, where her friends maroon Margot in order to give Eve her 'break', wouldn't have been the same without Celeste. 'She was perfect.' Celeste, however, did not return the compliment, complaining later that Bette and Gary Merrill spent all their time together and ignored everyone else. Bette ended up disliking her even more.

Bette admired Joseph Cotten – she found him easy to get along with and no threat to her star status – and she also liked Fred Astaire, Barry Sullivan, Paul Henreid, Steve McQueen, James Garner, James Mason, Henry Fonda, Ernest Borgnine, Alan Bates and Sterling Hayden. She thought Charlton Heston was boring, didn't like Cary Grant – although she would have liked to work with him – and was always very anti Charlie Chaplin.

When asked who her favourite actor was she nearly always said Claude Rains, and she also spoke highly of George Brent – with whom I suspect she had an affair. Brent came into her life early on at Warners at a time when the Howard Hughes affair had left her devastated. His sex appeal had led to a number of Hollywood conquests. He seemed solid, dependable and secure despite having a rather vicious tongue, but they were not emotionally suited. Brent was unable to cope with so much temperament, and was constantly annoyed by what he saw as her 'penny pinching'.

She liked many of the English actors and told me how impressed she was with Paul Scofield, whom she had recently met.

'I think he is the greatest English actor,' she told me, 'in terms of characterisations. He is my choice for the greatest. And I found out he was offered a knighthood many times but he wouldn't take it. He was very interesting the night I met him. He said, "I don't think knighthoods have anything to do with actors." '

She was not fond of Claudette Colbert, Irene Dunne or Rosalind Russell, but did like Jane Wyman. She was not particularly impressed by the young Ronald Reagan, who was always referred to as 'little Ronnie Reagan' at Warners.

When in her more scandalous moods, Bette would claim that there were two 'round holes' in Hollywood – Ingrid Bergman and Grace Kelly. She always claimed that coming off the soundstage at Warners one day she found Gary Cooper and Ingrid Bergman making love standing up against a back wall of the studio.

Bette was very fond of the great costume designer Edith Head, and she liked both George Arliss and Paul Muni, who were good to her when she was fighting to get established, and particularly Arliss from whom she learned much of her 'English style' of speaking. She found working with Mr Muni very difficult since his wife, Bella, was always sitting on the set, knitting. At the end of each take Mr Muni would look across for a nod or a shake of the head from Bella. If it was a shake, he would ask for a re-take.

She first met Arliss when he came to teach at her drama school. He later saved her Hollywood career after she had been fired from Universal Studios and was about to go back to New York. He was a strange-looking man, ugly, skeletal, round-shouldered with a beak-nose and alarming eyes, but his acting skills had made him a great power at Warner Brothers. He asked her to come and see him about co-starring in his film *The Man Who Played God*. He wrote in his memoirs that from the first moment he met Bette he clearly saw her quality: that she was the only actress he ever worked with who brought more vibrant responsiveness and interpretation to a part than was contained in the lines or was visible at first inspection.

Starring with the 'great lover' Charles Boyer was also a marvellous experience for her. One day she was working without him when she noticed a small, pot-bellied, bald man sitting on the set. She stopped working and demanded to know who this stranger was. To her embarrassment she was told it was Charles Boyer – without his wig, corset or lifts. He was an immensely popular figure at the time, very private and, like Bette, completely dedicated to his art.

She was an immense admirer of Carl Sandburg the poet, who had written some verses for her which she had framed on the wall, and of Somerset Maugham who had visited her on the set. She adored Spencer Tracy and James Cagney with whom she made *The Bride Came C.O.D.* During the making of the film Bette had to jump out of a plane onto the desert sand. She did as she was instructed, but sat on a cactus. She was in agony and had to have the spines removed by a doctor. The writers decided it was such a good routine that they included it in the picture, which won them a great deal of publicity.

She always told me that one of her great regrets was that she never got to star opposite Clark Gable. At one time it was suggested that she should play *Gone With The Wind* opposite Errol Flynn. She was so sure that Flynn would have been wrong for the part of Rhett Butler, that she turned down the film. Bette had been most happy with Flynn when they had made *The Sisters* together, but never thought of him as a great actor. Although Warner was rumoured to have told David Selznick he could have Bette for Scarlett as long as he cast Flynn as Rhett, Bette was not to countenance this deal. Again she was correct, and *Gone With The Wind* was saved. In 1939 Bette made *Elizabeth and Essex* with Flynn and every time she had to play a scene with him she would say to herself, 'Why isn't this Laurence Olivier?'

Robert Wagner and Natalie Wood were both to play parts in Bette's life. I first met Robert (R.J. as he is known to his friends) in Chamonix in the French Alps, many years before meeting Bette. I will be forever grateful to him for introducing me to Spencer Tracy who he was working with at the time on the film *The Mountain*.

Bette first met and liked Natalie when she was a young girl. Natalie was always afraid of the water, which is what made her death by drowning all the more horrible. When she was making a film called *The Star* with Bette, the director one day told her that she would have to drop into the water off a pier. Natalie had complete hysterics, but the director wouldn't change his mind. Bette, who was in her dressing room, heard the row and went onto the location to see what was happening. When she saw Natalie sobbing her heart out she said that the scene was to be struck out, or she would walk off the film herself. I believe Natalie was always grateful to her.

R.J. came into Bette's life when he offered her a part in *It Takes a Thief*, his successful television series, after he took over as a co-producer of the programme. He sent her a script and she accepted immediately. Fred Astaire had already guested on the show and Bette, who had liked R.J. on the screen, was happy to follow in 'Astaire's shoes'.

R.J. enjoys the company of all the great Hollywood legends, and he knows just how to treat them. Bette had been trying to adjust to the changes in the industry, but R.J. was happy to lay on full star treatment for her. There was a gold name-plate on her dressing-room door and fresh flowers were delivered daily. She was addressed as Miss Davis by everyone, and shown the sort of respect which she deserved from all members of her profession. His attitude paid dividends for him, because he was able to charm Bette into doing things which other producers and directors would have found impossible. At the end of a particularly gruelling day's shooting, Bette announced that enough was enough, and retired to her dressing room to get ready to leave. It was found to be necessary to do one more shot, and R.J. set forth to persuade Bette to co-operate.

'I'm not doing it, R.J. No way,' she said, adamantly. 'I can't, I'm too tired.'

In the old Hollywood days, when everything was done in the studio, they could always hold a shot over until the next day, because the set would still be there in the morning. R.J. had to explain to Bette that this was television, and that it would not be possible to do the shot any other time. 'You simply have to do it, Bette,' he told her, and for him she did it.

They went on to become firm friends and I often dined with Bette and R.J. She certainly liked R.J. more than Natalie, who could sometimes behave very strangely. Bette often asked guests at her parties to wear name tags, a bit like delegates at business conventions. She would write them out in advance, and at one party she wrote 'Natalie Wagner'. Natalie made an enormous fuss about it, refusing to wear it and saying that her name was Natalie Wood, and everyone knew her anyway.

At another dinner party R.J.'s mother, Chattie Wagner, was there, and it was obvious that Natalie resented her mother-in-law, although Bette and I both found her charming. When it came to the end of the meal they were about to leave when Natalie refused, point-blank, to allow R.J. to give his mother a ride home with them, even though she lived at the Bel Air Hotel which was not far from their house in Beverly Hills. I was happy to oblige Chattie with a lift, of course, and we became good friends.

I can remember the exact moment when R.J. told me that he planned to re-marry Natalie. We were driving round Hyde Park Corner in London, in my battered old mini. I very nearly ran into another car I was so surprised.

'Why?' I asked.

'I can't help it, Roy,' he said, 'I love her.'

Because she was so fond of R.J., Bette was delighted to come to England to work on a film for him called *Madame Sin*, some of which was made on location in Scotland. Towards the end of the filming they had considerable budget problems and R.J. had to use his charm yet again. This time he told Bette that there were still a few days' extra filming to be completed after her time on the set was up, although she obviously featured in the scenes. It basically meant that she would be giving her services for this extra time. For the sake of the film, and for R.J., Bette agreed.

At that time R.J. was dating Tina Sinatra who, being the daughter of Frank, was something of a princess. They both came to stay with us at Ascot and I will treasure the memory of Bette Davis taking breakfast on a tray upstairs to Tina Sinatra's bedroom. Tina didn't rise too early in the mornings and Bette served breakfast in the dining room at the usual time at weekends. Later the same morning Bette, R.J. and I were in the sitting room. They were talking private business matters, and I was reading a paper.

Bette suddenly stopped R.J. 'Just a moment,' she said, 'Roy's here.'

I looked up and realised that I was intruding. 'I'm so sorry,' I said, 'I'll go immediately.'

'That's all right,' R.J. assured her. 'I have no secrets from Roy.'

'I certainly don't mind if he stays,' Bette agreed.

Of course I left them in private, but they had made me feel good with their trust in me.

During the filming of *Madame Sin*, Rudolf Nureyev asked me if I could arrange a meeting with Bette for him. It wasn't hard to persuade her, since she was a great admirer of his. I arranged for a table at The Guinea, a restaurant in a secluded mews behind Bruton Street in Mayfair, for Bette, Rudi, R.J. and myself. The meal went very well indeed. Towards the end, however, a dozen of the most outrageous gentlemen swished across the restaurant, begging Bette for autographs. They had obviously been tipped off by Rudi that she would be there. This procession disrupted the whole restaurant and, of course, started all the other diners sending their menus over to be signed. Bette signed with good grace, but I could see that she was saving up her energies for a just revenge.

As we went outside to our cars, they were saying goodbye. 'It has been so lovely, Rudi,' Bette purred. 'Next time we meet it must be in your dressing room because, you see, I've never seen you dance.'

She meant, of course, that she had only seen him on film and television, but it was neat revenge, and Rudi was quite obviously shaken and annoyed.

During the filming of *Madame Sin*, the gossip columnist Radie Harris visited the set at the insistence of Robert Wagner. I told Bette that Radie had asked in one of her columns why Bette Davis was always escorted by homosexuals. Bette was incensed when she heard this and became party to a little plot. Harris was wearing a pink coat which I ceremoniously took from her when she came on set. When she called for her coat approximately forty minutes later to leave the studio, it returned black and damaged. The tea boy had been instructed to do his best to it!

Another visitor to the set was Bette's old friend and co-star Olivia de Havilland. The press were invited to take photographs of the two screen stars and when it was time to leave I escorted Olivia to her car.

'You see, Roy,' she said, 'She's Jesus Christ and I'm John the Baptist.'

Previously Olivia had commented to me: 'There is only one thing wrong with Bette Davis – she has too much talent.'

14

A Tough Professional

When I met Bette her career was not at its height. She had a theory that everyone goes through 'ten black years', a time when your professional and personal life just goes on the skids and you can't get anything to work for you. Both of us felt that we were in a period like that. I was just at the start of my career and fighting to get established. She had reached a peak undreamed of by most people, but she didn't seem able to get back up there as far as the work itself was concerned.

Bette, being a fighter, was no stranger to bad times and knew how to keep going even when everything seemed to be against her. In the 1950s, when work became scarce, Bette took an advertisement in *Variety* and other trade papers.

> Mother of three – 10, 11 and 15
> Divorcee, American, Thirty years'
> experience as an actress in Motion
> Pictures. Mobile still. And more affable
> than rumor would have it. Wants steady
> employment in Hollywood (Has had Broadway)
>
> Bette Davis c/o Martin Baum, G. A. C.
> REFERENCES UPON REQUEST

This was no joke, this was Davis at her real best, and it demonstrated her no-nonsense approach to her career and to life generally. She knew that only she could improve her situation, no-one else would do it for her. Some people in Hollywood saw the ad as evidence that Bette was on the slide, but fortunately her subsequent successes and the publication of her memoirs *The Lonely Life* proved them wrong.

Each year, when she sent me a Christmas card, she would put something to the effect of: 'Let's hope this is your year.' She understood exactly what I was going through, and I was, through various incidents, to get an idea of how hard life was for her as well, despite her immense success.

Hollywood is a very fashion-conscious business, and if the producers think that a star is out of favour with the public they won't go near her. Bette, of course, was never out of favour but the powers in the industry thought of her only as a character actress more suited to cheap horror movies or small guest parts where her name would still draw a large movie-going public.

In the early 1960s she had agreed to make a comedy in Italy called *The Empty Canvas*. Although she spoke her lines in English, all the other characters spoke in Italian. She told me that she thought it might be worth having the film dubbed into English for wider distribution. She asked me to go with her to a screening, at which she would show the film to her Hollywood agent Paul Kohner, and find out what he thought. He booked a screening room off Sunset Boulevard, near the 9000 block, opposite the agency's offices, and I took her there at the appointed time. Mr Kohner did not show up, so we started to run the film. He eventually arrived ten minutes before the end. Bette was obviously angry but she controlled herself, not wanting to fall out with him. When the film ended we went outside onto Sunset Boulevard. Mr Kohner said 'good-bye', turned his back and walked off to his office.

Bette Davis had been unceremoniously 'dumped' by her agent on Sunset Boulevard without a word of explanation or apology. No doubt Mr Kohner was more concerned with looking after the more fashionable clients on his books, like Charles Bronson. Watching Bette that day, however, I got a glimpse of just how long and hard a struggle it is to stay at the top. Neither of us said anything about the incident. We stood in silence for a second, drinking in what had happened, then I put my arm around her shoulders and took her home. Not long afterwards she found herself a better agent.

I do have to say, however, that she was wrong about *The Empty Canvas*. It would not have been worth dubbing into English. Although she did make a number of low-budget, low-grade horror pictures, both in America and Britain, she quite rightly turned down most of the scripts that were sent to her. She was always very open to the idea of doing television, even in the days when other Hollywood stars looked down on it as an inferior medium. She appeared in *General Electric Theatre, Alfred Hitchcock Presents* and *Perry Mason*. She sang and danced on *The Andy Williams Show*, and guest-starred in *Laugh-In*. She also agreed to make episodes of *Gunsmoke, The Virginian* and *Wagon Train*. She found television different from filming and suffered certain discomfitures that she had not been used to but she knew that it was the way of the future and she always hoped that she would find a vehicle for herself in a situation comedy. Many of the other stars of her era such as Jane Wyman have now managed to build amazing second careers for themselves on television, and Bette was aware of this possibility many years before the others.

She once told me that she had done thirteen pilots for series, not one of which was taken up. I think this was a slight exaggeration but she certainly did make a great many. She ran one for me in which she played with the actress Mary Wickes who had, years before, played the nurse in *The Man Who Came to Dinner*. Miss Wickes was a close friend of Lucille Ball. Bette decided not to like her.

It was probably just as well, however, that she did not get mixed up in a long running series. She would have been totally unfit temperamentally for the work. Bette Davis was a great star. She was used to being made a fuss of, of being someone special, and was a perfectionist in everything she did. Soap operas and sit-coms are made by extremely hard-working teams of people, who are cooped up together for long periods of time, often turning out work of a less than perfect standard. The ability to get on with others and to work fast is often the most important factor. The speed would have been quite unsuitable for her – although many of her great films had been made within a month – and she would have become bored with the subject matter very quickly, wanting to move on to new characters.

Bette would never have been able to fit into one of these repertory teams. She was altogether too large a character and too volatile. She would have taken a dislike to someone else in the cast or on the team, and would have waged a dreadful vendetta against them, or she would simply have created an unpleasant atmosphere for everyone in attempts to get her way over some minor matter.

In her early days in Hollywood, of course, they made films under the most appalling conditions and at a frantic pace, but Bette was younger then. Nevertheless she had suffered badly from her nerves as a result of the pressures. The studios did not have luxuries like air conditioning when she first arrived. The soundstages were often completely sealed off, even down to the ventilators, in order to prevent noise penetrating from outside. The California heat, multiplied by clumsy arclights, could reach unbearable levels.

Many of the studios, including Warners, owned their own theatre chains or had interests in cinema chains all over the world, and made pictures as fast as they could to feed the hungry screens. Sometimes they even had to shoot 'back to back' which meant the stars were doing one picture in the morning and another in the afternoon.

Because Bette had such a reputation for being a monster, many people were extremely surprised when they actually worked with her for the first time. Having been told by everyone they met that she would steal their scenes, hog the spotlight, re-write the scripts and try to take over from the director, they would often be surprised to find a totally professional and kind woman. Bette, more than any other star, made pictures back-to-back.

The day before beginning shooting on *All About Eve*, the writer and director Joseph Mankiewicz received a call from Edmund Goulding who had directed Bette in *Dark Victory*.

'Have you gone mad, dear boy? How could you hire such a woman? She will destroy you. She will ground you down to fine powder and blow you away. You are a writer, dear boy. She will come to the stage with a thick pad of long, yellow paper, and pencils. She will re-write everything and then she, not you, will direct. Mark my words.'

Fortunately Mankiewicz was not put off and found that Bette was a dream to work with. How she behaved always depended on whether she liked and respected the people she was working with. If she thought they were idiots she would do everything in her power to get rid of them. If that failed she would try to do their jobs for them. But if she liked and respected them she would do anything for them. She explained her feelings to Mankiewicz:

'I am neither Lady Macbeth nor Portia; I'll play either at a drop of a hat, anywhere. If I make a horse's ass of myself on the screen it is I – me, Bette Davis – who is forty-feet by thirty-feet horse's ass as far as the audience is concerned. Not the writer, not the director, the producer, the studio gateman, nobody but me. I'm up there as a representative horse's ass for all concerned. I made up my mind a long time ago, if anybody is going to make a horse's ass out of me, it's going to be me.'

Mankiewicz was extremely impressed. He wrote:

On the first day of shooting, I was marking Eddie Goulding's words. I had my antennae deployed to pick up possible storm warnings. Miss Davis arrived on the set fully dressed and made up, at least a quarter of an hour before she'd been called. She didn't even glance at the set. She lit her cigarette and opened the script – not, as I noticed at once, the scene we were doing that first morning . . . She was letter perfect. She was syllable perfect. There was no fumbling for words; they'd become hers – as Margot Channing. The director's dream, the prepared actress.

One director whose work she did admire, but with whom she could never work, was George Cukor. George was one of the three greatest directors in Hollywood. He was a wonderful, plain man with thick lips and a foul tongue. He was particularly well-known for his work with women. He had directed Hepburn, Garbo, Crawford and virtually everyone except Bette. When *Gone With The Wind* was being filmed Clark Gable had him fired, but both Vivien Leigh and Olivia de Havilland told me that they 'phoned Cukor almost every night to ask what they should do with their scenes for the next day's shooting.

Many years before, George had directed a stock company in upstate New York. Bette had joined as a young actress and George had fired her. Why he did so is not known, although many people believe he gave in to pressure from the rest of the company who found Bette's puritan obsession with work at the expense of all else very hard to take. She was not popular with her fellow players even then. Bette never forgave George for getting rid of her. Every time she came across him she would bawl him out: 'You fired me!'

I knew George quite well and one evening I suggested to him that he should bury the hatchet and make a film with Bette. He agreed that it would be great, since he would have liked to add her name to his roll call. When I next saw Bette I told her that I thought she should make a film with George, and that he was willing to talk about it. The next time I saw George, however, he told me that they had met at a dinner party and all she had done was berate him all over again for firing her all those years before. 'Who needs it?' he asked. 'Fuck her!' It was an attitude which many people in the business ended up taking towards Bette.

When she was working with Sir Michael Redgrave on *Connecting Rooms*, she told me how much she admired him as a great British actor, even though he was going through a very bad patch. One night, when they were supposed to be filming at Earl's Court tube station she waited with the crew until the early hours of the morning, but Sir Michael never showed up. In other scenes he was so ill she had to literally carry him through the scenes with her shoulder under his arm. She visited the Redgrave family at their home, and was rather taken aback by the fully grown – and very tall – Vanessa Redgrave, who came into the room after dinner and curled up on her father's lap. Although she always thought Vanessa was also very talented, she strongly disapproved of the way she used events like the Oscars to make her political points. At the end of the film, however, she was still as enamoured of Sir Michael as she had been at the beginning. She liked all the knights of the British theatre, with the exception of Alec Guinness. She worked with him on *The Scapegoat* when he had hoped to persuade Norma Shearer out of retirement for the part. She found him a 'rude, cold, heartless man'.

Whenever Bette was working she treated the job with the utmost seriousness and respect, even when the movie in question did not merit respect from anyone. This is what had always marked her out from other stars, who managed to combine their work with a sort of party atmosphere. Bette was something of a puritan when it came to her professional life. When she was filming *20,000 Years in Sing-Sing* early in her career, her character was supposed to have a car accident. They did the usual Hollywood make-up job on her, which meant bandaging her head like a nun and giving her one flattering black eye. She was furious and disappeared from the set. She went to the hospital and asked them to make her look like she had just had an accident. They made a really realistic job of it, so much so that when she drove back through the gates the guard rang up to the studio bosses to tell them the terrible news that their star had smashed her face up. It was all part of her determination to look for truth in her characters. Later actors like Dustin

Hoffman were to carry these ideas forward until they became ridiculous, with Hoffman staying up all night to appear as if he had done so in a scene from *Marathon Man*. Laurence Olivier, appearing in the same film, observed to Hoffman 'Why don't you just act it?' Dustin himself told me the story. And why did that fine actor Robert de Niro have to add so much weight for *The Raging Bull*? Bette, like Olivier, is an actor, and not a disciple of 'The Method'. She will add or subtract to her person whatever is required, but at the end of the day's work, she will be Bette, the make-up scrubbed away.

When making *Elizabeth and Essex* in 1939, for instance, she spent many hours working out the correct make-up with the make-up artist Perc Westmore. In the end she agreed to shave off much of her hair in order to achieve the correct look, and even had her eyebrows shorn. She went through the costumes stitch by stitch, jewel by jewel, comparing them to royal portraits dug out of the files by researchers. Every day she would get to the studios at 5.30 in the morning to spend two or three hours being made-up and dressed. Despite the fact that the costumes were horribly hot and cumbersome with layer upon layer of stiff brocade, high starched lace collars and heavy jewellery, she insisted on wearing everything, even when the director wanted her to compromise.

The night before working she would always be in her bedroom by nine o'clock, even if it just meant putting her feet up in front of the television or gossiping with me. She would then prepare everything for the following day, laying out the clothes she would need, the underwear, the script, her cigarettes and matches, and she would ensure she knew all her lines before she walked onto the set. It all stemmed from her upbringing. The one thing her mother had taught her when she started out on the road to stardom, was the necessity of planning, punctuality and all the other puritanical ethics and discipline which go into the production of great work.

She always needed to know that she was in control of everything, which meant that although she had to allow other people to do her packing for her, she would sometimes be reduced to hysterics because something had been placed in the wrong case. She always had to supervise everything. The need to be in control was a key to her personality. It was said that she didn't even like visiting the dentist or hairdresser because it meant she was in someone else's hands.

In England on mornings when she was working we would know better than to speak unless she spoke to us while she was having her breakfast – probably a boiled egg and toast – as we knew she was preparing herself for the day. Once in the studio she would be the same, although she would allow pop music to play on the radio while she was being made-up and dressed. All through the working day she behaved in the same way: the filming had to come before everything, although there were certain people, like myself and my mother, who she would go to great trouble to attend to when we visited her at the studio. She would always make my mother sit in the 'Bette Davis' chair, for instance, and she would insist that she herself placed it where my mother would get the best possible view of the filming. She would also become very irate if anyone else tried to do anything for my mother, wanting to do everything herself.

She never, ever had a drink while she was working. Her main preoccupation was always the work in hand. She would not even use her own private toilet if it meant she had to walk off the set for longer than necessary, but would use the same one as all the other women on the floor.

She liked to feel that she was working with directors who knew what they wanted and would tell her what to do. Unfortunately, her reputation as a monster frightened many of them off and others assumed that they would not need to give her much direction since she was Bette Davis. In the latter cases she often felt she was being ignored and not being given enough attention, which would bring out a protest for consideration. In the former cases she would simply take over the directing from them, in a subtle, professional manner whereby the director was never made to look anything other than *the* director.

There is no question that Bette lost work because of her reputation. When there are so many actresses crying out for work, why should directors and producers go looking for trouble? The problem is that great talent is often trouble, and many films – *Harold and Maude* for instance – might have been Oscar winners if they had only had the courage to cast Bette. I had asked Hal Ashby to take the brilliant Colin Higgins screenplay directly to Bette. I wish that he had, although the film he made is still wonderful.

132

Bette always wanted to find directors who could dominate her and to whom she could submit, but as she grew older and more awe-inspiring the number of directors who were her match became fewer. Even at the height of her reign in the Hollywood studios there were only a handful of men who dared to stand up to her. When Hitchcock was casting *Torn Curtain*, I was representing the great Austrian actress Elisabeth Bergner, known as the Garbo of the stage, and also as possibly the most temperamental of all working actresses. (That's why she hardly ever worked.) Hitch wanted her but finally declared that he did not want the trouble that would inevitably have gone with her. Bette was increasingly being recognised in this kind of league though, in all fairness, she would never have caused the kind of dramatic havoc that was totally peculiar to Elisabeth Bergner.

The two actresses also had something else in common. In the 1930s, when Bergner and her producer/director husband Paul Czinner, escaped from Nazi Germany and came to England and phenomenal success, they filmed *A Stolen Life* which co-starred Bergner with Michael Redgrave. It was a great success. About a decade later in 1945, when Bette decided to go into production, she chose *A Stolen Life* as her first vehicle. Bette chose Glenn Ford to play opposite her in this rather old-fashioned story of twin girls, one good and one bad, both played by Bette. She gave equally as fine a performance as Bergner, but the film was only moderately well-received.

Bette particularly disliked the use of locations and yearned for the old days when everything was done on the Warners backlot. She hated Egypt, where she went to film *Death on the Nile*. Although she loved the other people involved she found the country hot, unhealthy and inconvenient. On arrival in Cairo she said the streets stank and the noise kept her awake at night, but she did enjoy the beauty of the Nile and the Pyramids.

'In the old days,' she said, 'they would have brought Egypt to me.'

She was very excited about the prospect of working with Peter Ustinov, David Niven, Angela Lansbury and Maggie Smith. When she flew in from America to London for the pre-production work, she arrived at the Hyde Park Hotel, exhausted, and immediately attended eight costume fittings. She never traded on her age or her star status in order to get special treatment. During the filming she became particularly fond of Norton Knatchbull, the son of the producer Lord Brabourne, who looked after her so kindly. Norton, grandson of the man Bette and I admired so much, Earl Mountbatten of Burma, is now Lord Romsey and will some day become the second Earl.

She always had a love/hate relationship with live theatre. It was, of course, where she had started, and she loved the direct contact with the audience while fearing it at the same time. She found it very gruelling. Whereas many of the great stars of her era found second careers by going back into the theatre, Bette's nerve failed her. At the beginning of her career she had had to struggle hard to get as far as Broadway. When she finally made it, Ginger Rogers and Ethel Merman were opening in another show on the same night, and Bette's play folded soon afterwards.

'I hate the theatre,' she once told me. 'It's too tough a life at my age. Eight performances a week leaves you no time for a life of your own. Your heart thumps all day long, thinking of your performance that night. You finish at eleven or eleven thirty, and then that's the only time of the day you relax. So you stay up half the night, then you stay in bed half the next day. It's the most selfish, ridiculous life in the world.'

In 1952 she was approached to appear in a musical revue called *Two's Company*. The show involved her singing and dancing, neither of which are her greatest talents. At the time she was developing trouble with her jaw and didn't take the time to have it seen to, so that was making her ill and adding to her problems. Her commitment and intensity, and the problems of pushing herself to sing and dance well enough, ruined her health. The show opened in Detroit and the first scene involved Bette entering in a magician's box. It was airless, cramped and hot and when Bette burst out of it she felt giddy. As she went into her first number she blacked out, fell forward and hit her chin. Gary Merrill, who was then her husband, rushed onstage and helped her up. She struggled to her feet and walked out to the audience.

'Well, you can't say I didn't fall for you!' she announced.

When she finally agreed to have an examination it was found that she had osteomyelitis, a rare disease of the bone. It required a major operation in which the diseased tissue would have to be scraped from the jaw. If it had not been done perfectly, she could have ended up badly deformed. Bette went to see three different surgeons before deciding which one she trusted with the delicate task. Her choice was a wise one, and her jawline showed no sign of the serious operation that had been performed on it.

Yale University approached Bette with a request to take a masterclass in acting. Her fear of audiences made her decline, although she considered the offer seriously first. She was not impressed by some of the soul searching which the young method actors indulged in on the stage. In *Night of the Iguana* Christopher Jones, who, with James Farentino was one of the boys lazing in hammocks when she entered, asked the director what his motivation was for tying his shoe lace. Bette snapped out, 'For goodness sake, just tie it!'

There were other problems involved with her appearing on stage as well, because we often talked about arranging a vehicle for her in the West End of London. Her enormous popularity meant it was impossible for her to have an understudy. People who had paid to see Bette Davis were not going to be satisfied with some unknown playing her part. Managements were consequently very reluctant to take the risk of Bette being ill for a few nights – as she often had been in her career. We even sat down together to work out if she could shoulder the financial losses herself should some of the shows have to be cancelled, but it was quite out of the question. She then concluded by saying to me that she had had it all and did not need the 'glory' of the West End.

Many of Bette's illnesses, which caused her to leave film sets and shows, were psychosomatic, caused by her nerves. She was constantly worried about her throat closing up. If she wasn't getting her own way over something, she tended to develop flu or lose her voice for a few days. She seemed genuinely ill, but the ailments always cleared up when the problem had been solved by someone like B.D., Peggy or Harold Schiff and, on occasion, myself.

She had a very real fear that she might be the target of an assassin. Anyone so famous, who is up on a stage at a widely advertised time, is likely to feel vulnerable. When she first voiced these fears to me I thought she was being over-dramatic, but subsequent events in which famous people have been the target of assassins have shown that she wasn't being so unrealistic.

The other problem with live performances was that the audience wouldn't let her get on with the part she was supposed to be playing. Whenever she made an entrance the applause would be so sustained and ecstatic that it would be impossible for anyone on the stage to get their lines out. When she was appearing in *Night of the Iguana*, her co-star Margaret Leighton became infuriated by this. Every time Bette's character, the bad-tempered Maxine, made her entrance an enormous roar would go up from the audience, with much less excitement when Miss Leighton entered later. In the end the director and Tennessee Williams had to arrange for her to come on stage, pour a drink, light a cigarette and come out of character to take a call, before the play could continue. Margaret Leighton thought this most unprofessional, and neither woman spoke to the other unless absolutely necessary. The cast and crew divided into two camps: the 'pro-Leighton' and the 'pro-Davis'. The crew were mostly with Bette and the cast with Miss Leighton. Bette always made a point of winning over the crews both on film sets and in the theatre. She would get to know their first names, their marital statuses and how many children they had. She would always be approachable to them, because she knew how important they were to the way her performance was presented.

A great story was told to me by 'Binkie' Beaumont, the British impresario. On the last night of the show, when Bette was leaving the cast to be replaced by Shelley Winters, Bette started receiving telegrams from Miss Leighton. The first one said how nice it had been to work with her and how she wished she could do it all over again. The next one was even warmer in its praise, and by the third Miss Leighton was declaring something of a passion for Bette. The atmosphere when they passed backstage was still like ice, although, unknown to Bette, Miss Leighton had been receiving identical telegrams signed 'Bette Davis'. It eventually transpired that they were all being sent by Noël Coward because, 'They are two such silly bitches.'

She loved doing the one-woman shows, since they gave her the best of both worlds. She didn't have to worry about scripts or getting it right on the night, she could just go out there and have fun with the audience. She also enjoyed her Carl Sandburg readings with Gary Merrill and later Leif Erickson, but her theatrical career came to a sad end with Miss Moffatt, a part which certainly would have earned her a Tony award if events hadn't overtaken her.

Miss Moffatt was the central character in a musical play based on *The Corn is Green* by Emlyn Williams. The action had been moved from Wales to the Deep South with an all-black cast apart from Bette. Miss Moffatt was a school teacher preparing a particularly gifted boy for university. It was a wonderful part, and Bette had wanted to do it for a long time. The director, Joshua Logan, had a reputation for being difficult and for driving his actors hard. To coax Bette to accept the part, however, he wrote to her promising to behave himself and to make it a happy group. She had twelve copies made of the letter and kept one in each of her pockets and handbags. She wanted to have them on hand to show him should he need reminding. It did not work.

The show was going on tour, and Bette's name had sold out every seat available for six months in advance. Joshua Logan, however, had his eye on an eventual Broadway hit, and to this end they kept changing things from the first week and trying to improve the show, instead of giving it time to settle in. The pace was hopelessly fast, with pages of new dialogue being presented to the cast each day, and equally as many existing pages being withdrawn. Bette simply couldn't cope, and even began to mess up her lines on stage living in terror of new lines and new business. To cap it all she was beginning to suffer bad back pains. I arranged to go and see the show in Philadelphia and when her lawyer Harold Schiff heard that I was going, he asked me to do everything I could to dissuade Bette from leaving the show.

When I arrived in Philadelphia I met Vik for lunch at Bette's hotel suite while she was in the theatre, preparing for the matinée. From what he was not telling me, I could sense that something was wrong. He dropped me at the theatre later, but made some excuse not to come in. The show was marvellous, and Bette was great and it would have been a triumph all over the country, perhaps even on Broadway. But when I went backstage afterwards I was horrified to find her in tears. She was amazed to see me, not knowing that I was expected. She was racked with pain from a pinched nerve. To get her on the stage each night she was having to be laced into a vicious supportive corset. She was almost in a state of nervous collapse from exhaustion, and I could see that she couldn't go on much longer.

It was a sad end to what could have been a great stage comeback, and when it was all over she signed a playbill for the show, over which she wrote:

137

Roy,
Oh hell!
I loved doing this! Thank you for coming!
Love BD.

She later told me what it had been like.

It needed a lot of work, and the people in charge just weren't fair to me. They wanted twenty new pages by Boston in three days. Now this is impossible, absolutely impossible. I couldn't do it and I had brains enough to know it. They could have taken the show as it stood, never touched it, and packed it in for the rest of the tour. There wasn't a seat left. So they knew there was no need to change it. They were only worried about coming to New York a year from then, with great notices. It wasn't that great a script, it really was not. But we could have played that forever. But they wanted to change it, change it, change it, and I just couldn't do it.

That's what's happening with the theatre. We were on to Boston, for instance, we had two weeks sold out and they didn't need to change anything. Well, I finally froze the show for four nights, and we had a ball. We had a ball. But they just kept writing and writing and writing. This is what happens on the road. This is what was tragic. Nobody can do changes that fast. I had to get out.

Some of her greatest film roles came to her as second or third choice. Although she was often the obvious person for the part, the producers tried to find someone else first because of her reputation for being so difficult to work with. For *Now, Voyager!*, when she was actually under contract to Warners and they consequently wouldn't even have had to pay for her services, she had to fight tooth and nail to win it and only got it after Irene Dunne and Ginger Rogers had both turned it down. She argued that the film was obviously hers – so why didn't she get it first time round? The studio actually brought in other actresses, such as Ida Lupino, to threaten her and to try to tame her which, if they had succeeded, would have robbed the screen, and Warners, of its most vibrant personality!

'Ida Lupino was brought in to threaten me,' she said to me. 'Ha!' After a moment's thought she added, 'But she did get *The Hard Way*. I don't know how that one slipped away from me.'

She had to fight for all her roles and she didn't always win. Her three greatest regrets were losing *Gone With The Wind* to Vivien Leigh, and *Who's Afraid of Virginia Woolf* to Elizabeth Taylor and turning down *A Streetcar Named Desire*. The great mystery to me was where she actually found the depth of character which she put into her great performances. In the whole fifteen years that I spent with her I was never able to see an intellect or depth of human understanding that could have been capable of producing such great interpretations of such a wide range of characters. When I looked through her old scripts I noticed masses of hand-written notes, except in *All About Eve* where there were only one or two underlinings. Yet the power and range of her work is its own testament. She understood every single word and nuance of every character she ever played.

Not everyone realised just how nervous she could be, on film sets as well as live stages. On the first day of filming for *Madame Sin*, in 1971, her first scene was to be shot in Windsor Great Park. She had to allow a falcon to land on her arm, which terrified her. When she turned up on location the director, David Greene, acknowledged her and said, 'I'll be with you in a minute.' He went on with what he was doing for a while and then turned to her.

'Are you all right, Miss Davis?' he asked.

'No, Mr Greene,' she replied, 'as a matter of fact I am not all right. Feel my hand, Mr Greene. The palm is wringing wet. I'm very nervous.'

Because of her reputation for being a great professional star, directors did not always realise that she needed the same consideration as any other performer. The director Frank Capra had an unhappy experience with Bette while making *A Pocketful of Miracles* and later analysed where he had gone wrong.

It was all impossible. I 'lost' the picture right from the beginning. I realise now I should have understood Davis better. I didn't see that she was very sensitive, that she needed consolation and reassurance after so long away. I couldn't see that she was in fact vulnerable, living on her nerves. She'd only

139

become a monster to take care of herself in a monstrous business. Underneath she was a thin-skinned woman, deeply afraid and uncertain of everything except her genius. Her armour must not be penetrated and the fact that I tried appalled her.

It is generally believed in Hollywood that big stars achieve barely seven years at the top, and then start a slow decline in their careers. Bette Davis had eighteen prime years at the very top, and has been a major force for nearly fifty years. There were bound to be times when she did not get the vehicles which she deserved. I wish that she had stopped work earlier and allowed herself a more graceful retirement. I believe that the Emmy she won for the television film *Strangers* (1978) should have been her swan song. After that the decline started, when her famous voice and enunciation began to become mannered, almost like an impersonation of herself.

She was cast in *Strangers* as the reclusive mother in a small town, whose daughter (played by Gena Rowlands) returns after twenty years' absence. At first there is antagonism, with the daughter trying to win the mother over. We then find out that the daughter is dying of cancer but instead of receiving the sympathy and warmth which she was hoping for, the mother reacts with anger and revulsion. Bette went on to make *White Momma*, directed by former child star Jackie Cooper, and several less memorable films. The worst thing she did, I believe, was *Right of Way*, with James Stewart, but she desperately wanted to work with him and would have taken any script which allowed her such an opportunity. All through her career Bette complained that she wasn't given strong leading men to play against. Because he knew that she could carry a film on her own. Jack Warner did not waste his male stars on her pictures but used them to hold up other films. That pattern continued right up till the end. In James Stewart she saw the last of the great Hollywood men and she wanted to play opposite him. They had never worked together previously. The result was quite ghastly, however, because of the schmaltzy script.

She was often disappointed by the men who were chosen to play opposite her. While filming *Elizabeth and Essex* with Errol Flynn, the two of them did not get on at all and Bette ended up hitting him very hard during one scene. The blow actually made Flynn physically sick and he sent word from his dressing room that if she hit him again in the next take he would break her neck. She came perilously close but did not make contact next time around! She was always, however, full of praise for Flynn's performance with her in *The Sisters*.

She never liked leading men who did not accord her the respect which she thought she deserved. Flynn, who was notorious for his flippancy about acting and actresses, tried to be flirtatious with her, which did not go down well. While she was giving everything she had got to the creation of her character, she couldn't believe Flynn's behaviour – forgetting lines, yawning off camera at her when she was playing hers, pinching her bottom and making rude gestures at her. The angrier she became, the more he laughed at her.

One evening, when we were watching on television a film she had made called *Winter Meeting*, on which she was also the producer, she looked sadly at her co-star Jim Davis and said, 'To think I could have had Widmark.'

Many years later she came across Oliver Reed, who is no respecter of anyone. She told me how one night, after filming, she went to her hotel window to see what was causing a noise outside and found a woman swinging back and forth, upside-down in space. Reed had hired an acrobat and his wife to perform the trick. Bette was very shocked and not at all amused. On other nights she locked herself firmly in her room as Reed careered up and down the corridor outside on a waiter's trolley, calling out to her to let him in. But Reed was hardly in the category of actor that Bette had played with all her life, and this was the beginning of her decline in films.

She liked actors who were as serious about their work as she was. When she was making *Elizabeth and Essex*, Charles Laughton, whose work she greatly admired, came to visit her on the set.

'I've got some nerve, Mr Laughton,' she confessed, 'playing a woman of sixty when I'm only thirty.'

'Miss Davis,' came his solemn advice, 'never not dare to hang yourself.'

It has been by daring to accept the challenges that Bette Davis has remained at the top for as long as she has. But although Bette Davis could command large fees for her talents, she never managed to become one of the 'super-rich' as many other stars had done. She simply wasn't interested enough in money for its own sake.

She always liked to be paid 'up-front', and was never interested in taking a piece of the action, which is the way that most of the stars built their fortunes. Even now at the end of her career she can command large fees for guest appearances. The producers all know that they can sell a Bette Davis first-time appearance coast to coast for American television, regardless of the quality of the material. Even a 'bomb' can earn its money back in a deal like that.

During her days with Warners, of course, she was on a salary, and although it was a lot of money at the time she had a host of people to support. There was her mother Ruthie, her sister Bobby and then both hers and Bobby's children. She was particularly fond of Bobby's daughter Fay who frequently seemed to get herself into difficulties, according to Bette. There would be a long, evening telephone call, after which Bette would say something to the effect of: 'Fay is in trouble again, she has written off the car.' She would pretend to be exasperated, but she always sent money and remained a faithful benefactress.

None of Bette's husbands made much money, with the exception of Gary Merrill, and Bette never managed to do more than stay afloat. I don't think she would have liked being married to a man with more money than her; she would have resented the power that their money might give them over her. She was extremely proud of the fact that she never took alimony from any of her husbands. She liked the idea of being the 'breadwinner'. It meant she could look the world squarely in the eye, and it meant that other people were dependent on her.

Although she became obsessed with money during her long battles with Warners, it was more for the principles involved than the actual cash. When it came down to it she was greedy for good parts and for the success which they would bring her, but not for the material rewards.

By the time I met her she was certainly wealthy and had a very nice lifestyle, but it never felt like I was in the presence of a 'rich' woman. She had to keep working if she was going to keep paying the bills. She told me once how she went to see Marlene Dietrich and met her backstage afterwards.

'She was this old, old woman,' Bette explained, 'and I said, Marlene, why do you go on? She replied, "Because I need the money." '

So it was with Bette, which explains why she was often forced to appear in films which were not worthy of her talent. She enjoyed being the breadwinner of the family and helping her various relatives but she also expected a certain degree of gratitude from them. She was never mean but she was careful with money. When she was staying in England on expenses she would prefer not to pay for the most expensive hotels if it meant she could keep the money for herself. I remember once she asked me to find her a house to rent so that she could move out of one expensive hotel. She later told me that by doing that she had saved enough to carpet Twin Bridges.

When she was in Hollywood, prior to buying the apartment, she would 'house guest' with generous friends rather than rent somewhere. In restaurants she would also be very careful with the menu. At the Chinese restaurant opposite the cinema in Westport she once suggested that Vik and I took doggy bags away with us when there was too much left over from the meal. On another occasion she very generously ordered two lobsters for herself and me, because she knew I liked it. She served the complete lobster up to me at dinner, and we used the utensils necessary to retrieve every last piece of meat out of the shell.

'This is expensive,' she said, 'and you're gonna eat it all.'

Although I felt sad that I couldn't show how fond I was of her with the sort of extravagant gifts that befitted her status, she always showed that she was more touched and moved by the small, genuinely given presents, than by the grand gestures from people who could easily afford to make them.

She did not spend much money on herself. Most of her clothes came off the peg from I. Magnins, an expensive but not exorbitant shop in Beverly Hills. A friend of hers who worked there would select a few things that she thought Bette would like and then take them to her to choose from. With things like nightgowns she would just buy inexpensive, comfortable things with no concession to glamour.

When it came to buying things for B.D. however, she altered her attitude completely. Nothing was ever too good for her daughter, and 'good' meant 'expensive'. B.D. once told her mother that she would like a bearskin rug. Bette called a shop and asked them to bring some samples up to the apartment in Hollywood to choose from. The salesman brought three rugs. One cost about

$1,000, one was nearer $2,000 and the third was about $3,000. Both Bette and I liked the middle-priced one best, but she decided on the most expensive one – because B.D. had to have the best.

15

Joan Crawford

The rivalry between Bette Davis and Joan Crawford became one of the legends of Hollywood, yet there was very little foundation for it. Both were strong women and, in the end, they fell out, but they both had enormous respect for one another's professional abilities. Although they are linked as a team in the minds of the public, they actually saw very little of one another.

Bette recalled in her book *This 'n That*, the time when she was making *Dangerous* in 1935. She claims she had a crush on her co-star Franchot Tone, who was madly in love with Joan. Apparently the lovers used to meet for lunch and Tone would return to the set covered in lipstick and keen to let everyone know whose it was. Bette claims she was jealous. Tone went on to become the second of Joan's four husbands.

Joan undoubtedly admired Bette. During their years together at Warners she would often ask Bette to dinner. Bette would smile charmingly and say that she and her 'beau' at the time would be delighted.

'If I wanted your fucking "beau" to come I'd ask him,' was always Joan's retort. 'I'm asking you.'

Bette, who kept a picture of Joan on the wall of her home, believed that she was the quintessential Hollywood star. She epitomised glamour, while Bette saw herself more as a serious actress. There were three actresses who Bette thought had the most marvellous faces: Hepburn, Garbo and Crawford.

In 1961 when Bette was in *The Night of the Iguana* on Broadway, Joan came backstage to see her. She said she had sent the novel *Whatever Happened to Baby Jane* by Henry Farrell to the director Robert Aldrich in Italy and Aldrich had bought the rights. She said that she thought she and Bette would be ideal for the parts of the two sisters. A few weeks later Aldrich made the approach and Bette invited him over to her townhouse on Seventy-eighth Street.

'I only have two questions to ask, Mr Aldrich,' she said. 'First, which part?'

'Jane, of course,' he answered, and Bette nodded, satisfied.

'Have you ever slept with Miss Crawford?' she asked next, knowing that if they had then Joan would be likely to get most of the best camera angles.

It took Aldrich several seconds to reply. 'Not for the want of her trying,' he replied eventually, and Bette accepted the part.

Because neither Joan nor Bette were considered 'bankable' at that time, Aldrich had a lot of trouble raising the money for the film. The project was finally rescued by Elliott Hyman at Seven Arts. The budget was under a million dollars and the film had paid for itself within weeks of release.

The film marked Bette's return to Warners after thirteen years, and Jack Warner decided to throw lunch for the two stars. Each spied on the other to see what they would be wearing. Joan was elaborately dressed in vivid colours. Bette upstaged her by wearing plain black.

At the beginning of shooting for *Baby Jane*, Joan asked Bette what colours she would be wearing, so that they could be sure not to clash. Bette replied sweetly that she would be wearing white so Joan could wear whatever she liked, knowing that the film was being made in black and white, something the greatly professional Crawford had overlooked. She also enjoyed telling the story of Joan's false breasts.

'Joan had three sets of tits,' she told me, 'small, medium and large, and for the final scene on the beach she put the large set on. I had to drag her along the sand, and it was like climbing over mountains. Nobody, however well endowed, has breasts which stick up when they are lying on their backs.'

While Bette was quite happy to make herself look grotesque, Joan wanted to look as attractive as possible. While Aldrich was trying to persuade Bette to calm down her more hideous make-up, he was also trying to persuade Joan to look a little less glamorous. Bette recalled later that he had to fight hard to persuade Joan to remove her nail polish. Apparently Joan said, 'You have taken everything else away from me. You're not taking away my nail polish.'

Joan was the widow of the ex-chairman of Pepsi-Cola, Alfred Steele, and used to have a glass of Pepsi beside her all the time. Most people suspected, however, that it was liberally spiked with vodka.

Bette was amused by Joan and often teased the other actress without her knowing. Joan would come to her to discuss her lines and Bette told me she would say, 'You're not really going to say that, are you Joan?'

'Why not?' Joan would ask.

'It's no good,' Bette would reply, and proceed to rip the pages out of Joan's dialogue.

Joan made no secret of her great professional admiration for Bette, and would always consult with her about professional matters, often agreeing with Bette's opinion. Aldrich was a strong character who didn't allow either of them to upset his schedule. The entire picture was shot in twenty-one days.

'Joan and Bette didn't fight at all on *Baby Jane*,' he remembered later. 'They behaved absolutely perfectly. They never allowed an abrasive word to slip out. They didn't try to upstage each other.'

The falling out came when the film was released. The two actresses were going to split the personal appearances at the 150 cinemas in the New York area where it was showing. Joan protested that Bette was getting the 75 best cinemas and withdrew her services. Bette took advantage of her withdrawal and did the whole tour. Their relationship never recovered. When Bette was interviewed during her promotion of the film, she told of how hard it had been for the producers to raise the money for *Baby Jane*, since no-one wanted to back a film starring 'two old broads'. Bette later received a stiff note from Joan instructing her not to refer to her as an 'old broad'.

When Bette was nominated for an Oscar, Joan was furious, particularly as the film had been made largely at her instigation, and she openly campaigned against Bette, despite the fact that an Oscar win would have added to the profits of the film and to Joan's cut from them. There was no doubt that Joan's was also a great performance and worthy of a nomination. She went to all the other nominees for the award and asked them if they would allow her to accept it on their behalf, should they be unable to attend the ceremony.

On the night of the Oscars Olivia de Havilland and Bette were sharing a dressing room. The two of them were chatting away about old times when a harassed little, grey-haired lady dresser came in.

'Miss Davis, Miss de Havilland, is there anything I can do for you?'

They felt sorry for her and told her they could manage themselves. She happily disappeared, leaving the two great actresses to 'zip one another up'.

'We got ourselves ready and tiptoed downstairs,' Olivia told me later, 'and as we passed the prompt corner at the side of the stage there in the middle was Joan Crawford surrounded by at least seven lady dressers, sewing on sequins, spraying, and all the rest.'

Bette told me that they then waited for the announcement of the winner, and when Anne Bancroft's name was called (for *The Miracle Worker*), Joan strode out to collect it on her behalf. As she passed Bette and Olivia, she let out a triumphant, 'Ha!'

The two actresses were re-united, albeit briefly, for the making of *Hush Hush Sweet Charlotte*. Bette had made a deal with the producers that she would work with Joan if they changed the title from *Whatever Happened to Cousin Charlotte* to *Hush Hush Sweet Charlotte*. They started work on location in Atlanta during a heatwave.

'Miss Crawford wouldn't take the charter plane down with us,' Bette told me. 'She went down on a scheduled flight. So when I arrived with the rest of the crew, there she was sitting in the hotel lobby, surrounded with 48 pieces of luggage. When she saw me she said, "Bette, would you believe it, they haven't got my room ready yet?" So I said to her, "Well Joan you are too early, you should have come down with the rest of us when you were expected." '

Bette was then ushered straight to her room and half an hour later there was a knock at the door.

'Bette, it's Joan.'

'Come in.'

Joan came in, looking perturbed. 'Bette, its awful, they've put me right next to the garbage disposal.'

Things did not improve in the afternoon, when they were doing some publicity pictures for *Life* magazine. The heat had become intense and they were called for three o'clock. When the car arrived at the hotel for them, Bette walked out to it. Turning to see where Joan was, she saw the great star walking down after her, with a man, bent double, walking backwards in front of her, squirting her legs with insect repellant. Joan managed to get to the car without being bitten, and they drove to the session, where the photographer wanted Joan to climb in and out of a jeep. Joan did not like to wear underwear. When it came to her turn to pose with one leg up on the jeep, the assembled company were horrified to see that her dress had clung to her every private crevice, leaving nothing to the imagination.

'Get the ass,' Bette whispered to Aldrich. Aldrich saw what she meant and explained the situation to Joan.

Three days later Joan had had enough and developed a diplomatic illness. It is widely thought that Bette had intended to drive her off the picture from the moment she arrived. Right at the beginning she said she didn't want to appear in any shots with the other star, which would have made shooting very difficult.

Both Peggy Shannon and I knew Joan before we knew Bette, and certainly few of the stories about her were exaggerated. She was, however, enormously popular with all the people whom she worked with. Whereas she could keep a devoted secretary for thirty years, Bette was lucky if they stayed for a week. In my view Bette was unquestionably the greater screen actress, but they were both the greatest of stars.

One evening, early in our relationship, when we arrived back at the Chantry, Bette decided she would make us some soup from a collection of cans. As she was stirring up the steaming brew, she seemed to be lost in thought.

'Roy,' she said at last, 'Why am I so good at playing bitches? I think it's because I'm not a bitch. Maybe that's why Miss Crawford always plays ladies.'

16

Return to Hollywood

When B.D. and Jeremy moved away from Westport to their farm in Pennsylvania, Bette was heartbroken. No matter how much trouble she gave B.D. there was no-one in the world she cared about as much. In 1977, she decided that it was time to return to Hollywood. She had already moved out of Twin Bridges and into a tiny cottage in Weston, Connecticut – even closer to B.D. and Jeremy's old home – which was a bad mistake. The cottage was very pretty but much too small for her. I stayed there a couple of times, but it was never as much fun as Twin Bridges.

Bette was not getting the work she thought she should be, and she needed to be closer to where film and television pilots were being made. She also reasoned that it would be no more difficult to reach B.D.'s new home from California than from Connecticut, but I think in truth she wanted to show them that she could manage without them. If they didn't want her, then she didn't need them.

Hollywood is really Bette's town. When she arrived in 1930 it was still pioneer country. The talkies had only just started, and actors and actresses were being brought in from New York to replace the silent stars who proved unable to make the transition into sound. Despite the enormous wealth of the existing stars, directors and producers, there was still little of the culture which makes city life enjoyable.

For the Easterners, the early Los Angeles was a salutary culture shock and many of them tried to escape the boredom and pressures through drink, drugs and other vices, while living in perpetual fear of being caught up in scandals that might destroy their burgeoning careers. Compared to New York and Broadway there was virtually no culture. Robert Benchley described Hollywood in 1930 as: 'A flat, unlovely plain, inhabited by a group of highly ordinary people, all of them quite at sea and usually in a mild state of panic in their chosen work, turning out a product which, except for certain mechanical excellences, was as unimportant and undistinguished as the mass product of any plant grinding out rubber novelties or automobile accessories.'

There were no speakeasies or cocktail bars and everyone was in bed by ten at night. This, however, was where the future was being created, and young actresses like Bette and Katharine Hepburn knew that. They were willing to put up with the indignities and discomforts of the place because they believed that movies could become an art form, and because they wanted to do good work. It was because of the efforts and skills of people like Bette that Los Angeles grew to be one of the major cities of the world. Now, of course, movies are only one of California's exports and it has become a state which is richer than the majority of the world's developed countries. The early movie stars, however, were the founding fathers, and as such they are revered and respected.

The modern denizens of Hollywood were delighted to have their queen returning home in 1977. They all wanted to meet and honour her. Dinah Shore wanted to make one of her chat shows into a tribute to Bette, having Jane Fonda and television star Peter Strauss on the same bill. Bette agreed.

One of Bette's most famous lines is, 'Peter, I want a divorce,' from her film *Payment on Demand*. It is largely memorable because of the emphasis which she puts on the name 'Peter'. All the impersonators pick up on it, and come on stage saying, 'Peter, Peter, Peter,' in exaggerated voices, which Bette doesn't understand at all. Dinah Shore had the idea that Bette should introduce Peter Strauss, perhaps saying, 'Peter, Peter, Peter!' in her inimitable way because Peter Strauss would enjoy it so. Bette didn't like the idea, claiming that she didn't say the name like the impersonators did anyway. In demonstrating how she really said it, she showed just how accurate the impersonators were, but I didn't say anything.

Bette didn't want to go through the main entrance of the studio, and elaborate arrangements were made for us to come in through the scene dock in order to avoid the fans.

The evening of the show was clear and warm. Bette and I arrived at the studio and while we were walking from the car one of the most unkempt of her regular autograph hunters leapt out at us. Bette, despite being startled, agreed to sign some autographs for him, and we went on into the studio.

In the dressing room we found that Dinah had left a gift of a bottle of Scotch for Bette. Although she wouldn't have dreamed of having a drink before the show, she was pleased by the gesture, and when Dinah came in to talk to her she only put up a few, feeble protests against saying 'Peter' and finally agreed. When she did it the audience howled their appreciation.

Now that she was moving back to Hollywood permanently, however, she couldn't 'house guest' with friends. She had to find a home of her own.

Roddy McDowell, the film actor, had tried for many years to persuade Bette to attend one of his dinner parties, but she had always eluded him. At this time I found Roddy a charming man, and used to enjoy going over to his lovely house for morning coffee and 'film talk'. He had a fantastic collection of films and was also a fine photographer. One day, however, when both Bette and I were in Hollywood, Bette rang to say that Roddy had invited her to dinner and that she had told him she would only go if I could take her. I said okay. A few minutes later Roddy McDowell phoned, unaware that Bette had just been on the line, and invited me to the dinner without mentioning the Bette Davis connection. I was not particularly flattered to know that I was only being invited to be Bette's chauffeur, but for her I was happy to do it. So for once, I graduated from coffee mornings to one of his famous and perfectly terrific dinner parties.

By this time Bette was becoming a very nervous passenger in the car, so I decided to drive the route the day before. It was over Laurel Canyon, and I wanted to be sure that I wouldn't miss the turning.

The evening went very smoothly. Joan Rivers was at the party, enormously nervous at meeting Bette Davis for the first time. She asked me what I thought she should say to such a great star. It is hard to imagine Joan lost for words. I told her to just be natural.

Roddy managed to become friendly with Bette during the evening and much later helped her to find an apartment on North Havenhurst, one block south of Sunset Boulevard, close to the site where the famed Garden of Allah used to stand. It is near the Chateau Marmont, a building reputed to be partly owned by

Garbo, where all of us have stayed at one time or another, including Bette in one of her less glamorous periods.

West Hollywood is a predominantly gay suburb, full of nice houses and old ladies who like the unthreatening atmosphere. It has its own lady mayor and is a separate city from the rest of Los Angeles, as is Beverly Hills. It wasn't exactly what Bette was used to. The fourth-floor apartment, however, overlooked 'La Ronda' where she and her mother first stayed when they arrived from New York with no money, no prospects and plenty of dreams. Bette enjoyed the irony of this.

The block, known as Colonial House, has an unassuming side entrance. Her apartment had large, comfortable rooms, which she furnished with all her favourite pieces, in exactly the same style as every other house she had ever lived in. It had twelve-foot ceilings which she found daunting. There was no hall, with visitors coming straight into the bright, airy sitting room. Her long trestle table was on the left, usually with an art book open on it, and lots of family photographs. Lattice doors, with an Oscar on the floor at each side, led into the dining room. It was like the house of a very successful character actor who is well settled for life – no more and no less.

Since I had my own place when I was in Los Angeles I didn't stay with her there, but I used to visit most days. Gradually, as her cocktail hour became earlier, I would find that we would have had dinner and she would be in bed by nine or nine thirty. I would then go off somewhere else for a second dinner with other friends. It made my social life very difficult. I never liked to rush her, so I could never give definite times when I could arrive at friends' homes to finish the evenings. All I could do was say I would try to get there between nine and ten. I began to worry about her, waiting outside her door after I left to hear her chain and lock it, sometimes having to shout back through to remind her. I also feared that she would set light to herself with her cigarettes in bed.

She managed to find out that the caretaker of the block was called Mr Lee, and she would plague him with complaints and problems. She would ring down, 'Is Mr Lee there? Then find him for me, this is Bette Davis.' In the end the poor man instructed his two assistants to also answer to the name Mr Lee, so that they could share the grumbles between them. Bette was bemused by the succession of apparently different Mr Lees, but never questioned it.

From her balcony you could see down to the swimming pool below. One day, Bette was leaning on the rail looking over at a corpulent man and his attractive family as they all swam and sunbathed.

'Look at that,' Bette shouted to me, loud enough for her voice to carry clearly down to the ground. 'Look at that disgusting man. It's revolting that a nice young girl and her children should have to be with such a fat, disgusting man.' I hoped they could not hear her and tried to stop her, but she pretended not to understand what I was talking about.

She was living here at the time of her seventieth birthday, and decided to throw a party for intimate friends. She wanted to give the party a 'black' theme, including a wreath on the door and herself in full black make-up and afro wig. She thought it was hilarious and insisted on answering the door personally to everyone. However, instead of falling about laughing, as she expected, most of the guests simply looked aghast at the horrifying sight.

At this time I had started my career as a journalist and writer, and a British daily paper had asked for an interview with Bette. It seemed like a ridiculous idea to me, since I knew her far too well to be objective, so I didn't pursue it. Some months later, however, she said to me. 'A friend of mine sent me an article you had written. It was very good. Why don't you interview me? It would be fun. Bring your tape recorder next time and we'll do it.'

For several weeks there were always reasons why she didn't feel like doing it that day. Eventually I just brought out my tape recorder and refused to take no for an answer. She agreed, climbed on to her chaise longue, put her feet up and waited for the questions. It was as if we were playing at being interviewer and interviewee.

'Miss Davis,' I began formally, 'we're in your new home, and it's April 1978, which is a very, very important month to you.'

'Yes, indeed. It's my birthday month and almost a week ago I was seventy years old, which is a staggering thing for me to realise.'

'But do you feel any different?'

'I don't think one ever feels any different, except one has the knowledge: the knowledge that the years go by, and the intellectual knowledge. I can remember when my mother was seventy and I thought "She's just had it, she's gone, it's the end of the world", but I'm sure she felt just as I do now. That's mentally of course, physically you know the difference. If only women could stop progressing physically at forty, and men could stop at fifty, but to go on progressing mentally, what a wonderful world it would be.'

This was the week of the Oscar ceremony which I had attended with her, so I asked if it was true that she had christened the award 'Oscar'.

'I think it's true,' she replied, 'although the Academy denies it. My first husband's middle name was Oscar, which I only found out the first time the ceremony took place. We both thought it was a horrible name, but the statuette's bottom really did look like my husband's, so that's what I called it. The Academy has been so angry about that.'

I asked her to describe the room we were sitting in for the readers.

'Somebody once said to me,' she recalled, 'that if I had furnished a tent in the Sahara desert they would know I was from New England. Most of the things here I've had for about forty years, with it all travelling back and forth across the continent with me – I think six times in all. It is all kind of Yankee, lots of pine and kind of inelegant in a funny way, but it's the sort of furniture I really love.

'This is a very old building, built forty-five years ago by Paul Williams, the great . . . the *first* Negro architect. It's very old-fashioned, and it's big and it's . . . well, I guess it's alright. The whole apartment is a kind of grey/blue and green, with a little bit of yellow and some red in the sunporch.

'It was a big thing for me to move from New England after fifteen years back to California. The children are all off somewhere, all married . . . I think this is what I should have done, come back here. I think I'm very glad I did. These ceilings seem very high, I think they must be twelve foot. They frighten me. Everything is finally done now, except the shutters, so I have started to invite people round. I've never had decorators, I always move myself. The biggest problem here was that I had so many pictures. Not paintings, pictures, and this place is a fortress – to get a nail into the wall of this old place was extraordinarily difficult – but it's done. It took me twelve weeks.

'I like to give my homes names, and I call this my Bailiwick West. I thought of calling it "What a Dump", but it's not and I thought that would insult it.'

155

She was about to take her one-woman show on tour in Southern California, and was leading a busy professional life generally.

'You still have perhaps the busiest professional life of any actor in the world,' I started.

'Of my age,' she agreed.

'I would think of any age.'

'No, but of my era. Yes, of my era this is true. I am about to start touring again. It will be the easiest tour yet, just on the West Coast, but I've always wanted to do it. The first tour was Canada and the Pacific North West, and the South. Then the next tour was Australia. Then there was England. I've always said I would do the West Coast. I enjoy doing the show, it's kind of fun. Then I'm going East to make a picture. Last year I made three films: a Disney film, a television thing and then went to Egypt for *Death on the Nile*. That was too much. But I think after I make the film *Strangers*, which I think is a smashing script, about a mother and daughter, hopefully that will be it for this year.'

On a recent trip to England she had made the record which had been such a disaster. I asked her about it.

'EMI never sold it to anyone,' she replied. 'Nobody ever heard it. I never have understood why. It was the heartbreak of my life that they never did a thing with it. It's a good record which makes me even angrier.'

B.D. had recently given birth to Justin, her second son.

'I have seen my second grandson,' Bette said proudly. 'I visited him for a day when he was just five days old. He's eight months now, so I simply can't wait to get back East to see him again. Next year B.D. and Jeremy will have been married fifteen years. They now have a lovely farm in Pennsylvania and live a life they really adore.'

I asked her if she would have allowed B.D. to become an actress.

'I would never have done anything about it if she had wanted to, but I couldn't be more pleased that she didn't want it. It's totally different for a young person going into the business today. I don't know how my mother lived through my early years in the theatre – the agony of your own child, will they be good or not? I was spared that.'

Bette had always said that her mother, Ruthie, had known that her eldest daughter was destined for something special the moment she popped her head out. I asked her about this.

'I think she always knew something was going to happen to me,' she said. 'She felt it much more than I did. She had a real hunch about me. One day, when we were living in a boarding house in Norwalk, Connecticut, she walked in and said "We're just going off to do something," and she took me into New York to the John Murray Anderson Dramatic School. She didn't have a dime. She walked into the office and said "I want my daughter to come to your school." Mr Anderson told me many years later he never knew why he accepted me. "It was just that woman," he said, "She simply overpowered me." '

'I've always been impressed by your library of books,' I said.

'Yes, I read every book I had, but I did not bring them all here. I have a whole section of my personal reading books in a library in Boston. Here I just have the current books and some that I adore.'

Everywhere Bette went she was also followed by all her memorabilia. She kept everything from her baby books to the scripts of her films, all bound in red leather. She always said that if she hadn't had a talent for acting she would have been a personal secretary. She was certainly very organised. I can imagine her as one of those fearful ladies who guard the privacy of their bosses with their lives – probably ending up a spinster. She did read a little during our time together, but I'm not sure quite how many of the books she actually finished.

'I keep everything,' she admitted. 'I really don't believe actors who say they don't keep anything.'

I questioned her about her interest in cookery.

'I have been known as a very good cook. It is my therapy. I don't paint china, I don't do needlepoint, I don't knit. I enjoy it because I think cooking is a kind of sharing. It also occupies all those months when I am not working. B.D. is a better cook than I. She can just start a meal at six o'clock and it all comes together. I can't do that, I'm a nervous cook. Cooking takes all my concentration, and it is a way of giving to other people. I could always cook a meal, even as a young woman, but I really started when I had the three children at home in Maine in the fifties.

'I'm a nester. Whatever hotel I go into I make a nest. They become my homes away from homes and I like to change the

157

furniture around a bit. I always travel with photographs of the family and the little knick-knacks that make it a home. I love most being at home with a few friends. In all people's lives there are a few friends.'

'And when you're at home, you like to be comfortable, and you like to wear things like men's shirts, don't you?'

'They talk about the new "Annie Hall" look. I've been stealing clothes from men for years – oversized sweaters, shirts, everything. I'd nearly always wear scarves or hats. I'm mad for hats. When you are working you spend hours on your hair and how you look, and it's much easier for me at home just to put a scarf on and a cap or a hat or whatever and not spend any time with how I look. I've always worn crazy hats – I have millions of them.

'I had a real Castro hat which I have given to my grandson. I paid $25 for it in an auction in Maine. Castro wore it, and my grandson has kind of taken over my love of hats, which is cute. He would come to my house when he was a very little boy in Westport and put on some of my hats. I had a cape and a Sherlock Holmes-type hat – that was his passion.'

Following the lines of the traditional film star interview, I asked her about some of her favourite things, starting with flowers.

'Daisies, freesias and lilacs. I suppose those are my three favourites. I'm very fortunate on my birthdays to receive all of them by the hundreds. With food I now tend to eat very, very simple foods, but I love everything. I think Italian food is probably my favourite, which I do not cook. I would rather go to a restaurant for something like a canneloni – it's a very tough food to cook. My favourite colours are red and yellow, particularly red.'

I suggested that she was a typical Aries – her birthday is on April 5th.

'I am definitely a typical Aries I think, but I am not very wise about astrology, although I think that people born under the same signs have basic characteristics in common. I do believe in astrology. I believe that when you have a chart done, which I have done now and then, there are sometimes months in your life when nothing's going to happen and there isn't anything you can personally do about it. It's just going to be a mess.'

'What is your opinion of the product of your industry today? Whose work do you like? I know, for instance, that you predicted

Richard Dreyfuss was going to win the Academy Award, and you were right.'

'I just think that his performance in *The Goodbye Girl* is without doubt one of the greatest performances I have ever seen from a young actor, and I am very proud of the Academy. They could have sunk into Mr Burton, who was nominated how many times?'

'Six.' (Richard Burton once told me that he knew he would never get an Oscar, because the industry could not forgive him for being married to Elizabeth Taylor.)

'I have a great respect for Mr Burton,' she continued, 'who has resurrected his career like you cannot know, but Mr Dreyfuss was the one who should have won. I haven't seen all the films which were nominated, so I cannot judge between Diane Keaton and Jane Fonda.'

I told her that Jane Fonda admired her more than any other actress, and Bette told me the story of how she had allowed Henry Fonda to leave the set of *Jezebel* in order to be there for Jane's birth.

'I'm very proud that she feels this way about me, and I feel the same about her, but I do not agree with the mixing of politics and business. Miss Redgrave is another one. She made such a fool of herself at the Awards. Now, she should have known from what happened to Marlon Brando and the Indian Lady years ago. The Academy is not a political deal. Granted, Miss Redgrave's performance was sensational, but then she should have known it was just for the performance. She was an absolute fool that night. Everyone was thrilled when she got the Oscar later.'

I asked her about William Wyler.

'I think he's the greatest director Hollywood ever had. The greatest editor, the greatest man who ran a camera, the greatest director of performances. Just the greatest, period.

'I have not worked with the so-called "new great directors", so I cannot give an opinion on them. They are so different today, because I think, you know, motion pictures are different. I think I might feel the same way about Mike Nichols because in *The Graduate* he kept all the old and incorporated the new.'

'You were President of the Academy for a while?'

'Yes, for a very short time. They didn't know I was a strong woman. I had many ideas, but they never let me get by with any of them, so I just left.

'I wanted a British theatre thing. I wanted the extra vote to go because they were all mostly foreigners, who couldn't speak English. If you gave them ice-cream every Saturday they voted for you. When Mr Hersholt became President he eventually got rid of the extra vote, but when I suggested it – out. When I suggested the Grauman's Chinese for the British War Relief at $25 a seat, they said I was wrecking the Academy. The dignity of the Academy of Theatre, and when I look at it today or watch it on television, I have to die laughing.'

I decided to touch on her reputation for tyranny.

'Unless you are known as a monster,' she explained, 'you'll never become a star. Unless you are known as a monster you have not made it.

'In fact I am not a monster, only with incompetents on the set. If I have an idiot director or an idiot fellow actor, then I'm a monster. The reputation is valuable. It will always be so. It is self-preservation because it is your name which is up on the screen. Willie Wyler, the greatest director of all, once said to a whole cast of people, "I don't care what goes on on this set. I don't care if we all hate each other, I only care what it looks like when that audience goes into that theatre." You see you can't put up sub-titles. "I was nice to this idiot director", because only the star of the film takes the blame, or the fame. I've fired directors, I've done many things, always for the good of the film.

'On *Madame Sin* I gave up my overtime for the film, for which my agent and lawyer could have killed me.

'It takes guts to be a monster because everyone loves to be loved. When I was at Warners I was working with the same crews for eighteen years. If I go to England to do a film with a whole new crew they quake, they shake, they die.

'I've had directors ask me to come down to the set early in the morning on the first day just to chat with the crew so they'll relax.

'I have had a terrific amount of luck in my career. With *All About Eve*, I only got the part because Claudette Colbert hurt her back. You can't ask for more luck than that. I've had scenes to play when I was a wreck or my voice had gone with laryngitis or something, which would make people think it was a great performance.'

I asked her if she thought there would ever be a fifth husband now.

'Oh never! Oh never!' she exclaimed. 'I don't think I would ever have the opportunity for a fifth. I don't want it. When I married Gary Merrill, who was my fourth, I had been a widow for some time after my second marriage, so it's basically three marriages – I said that if that didn't work, never, never again.' (This was Bette's way of explaining that she had only been divorced from three husbands, not four.)

'It was a love affair with Gary Merrill, though?'

'Definitely, definitely. I adored him. I think if Farney had lived that would have been *the* marriage. But you know I always had to do it the hard way. Yes I think that marriage would have been perfect, that would have been the one that lasted – no question.

'Every marriage is some kind of attraction at the time. I don't think anybody in the world marries if they don't think "This is it", but it doesn't mean it *is* it. I just had ill luck. I had a marvellous doctor say to me once, "You mustn't be embarrassed about all this. You just had ill luck." I think that anyone who has a long, long marriage has the greatest luck in the world. I think divorce should be allowed. You shouldn't spend your life with something that's driving you mad. When I signed the paper for B.D. to be married at 16, which was hard to do, I said, "If it doesn't last, she can only learn from this", and she's very lucky it did. It's terrific luck.'

I suggested to her that the American public looked upon Hollywood people as their royalty.

'The only royalty we ever had were motion picture people,' she agreed. 'They were the kings and queens here, and millions of people – darling little people – need kings and queens.

'I don't think it is so much the case today, except for some of the oldies. Certainly I still receive the same respect, and John Wayne and Jimmy Stewart and Henry Fonda. So many have gone.'

'Miss Davis, you are unquestionably the queen amongst your peers. Who would you nominate as king in the talking pictures?'

'Gable, Cooper and Tracy in two different areas. Tracy in the acting area, the other two in the motion picture area.

'But I never personally – and you have known me a long time, Roy – I do not personally think of myself privately as being famous in any way.

'The Life Achievement Award from the American Film Institute was the frosting on the cake for me. I appreciate my two little Oscars, no question about it. If your own industry votes for you, that's beautiful, and I've been nominated ten other times. A couple of times I should have won and didn't. One was *Baby Jane* and one was Margot Channing in *All About Eve*. There was also *Dark Victory*, but that was the year of *Gone With The Wind*.

'Very often the Academy has given Special Awards, when they know somebody is dying, and sometimes the people haven't made it, like Eddie Robinson. I trust that never happens to me – I would hate it, and my daughter would have to fly out here and accept it because I was dead by the time I got it. No, I don't want special awards.

'When you go to an Oscar show or an AFI Show and you get the sort of reception I get, of course I am honoured, and I do not ignore it and I do not say "This is nothing". I am very grateful that this has happened to me. I have been working fifty years and I am very proud of it, but there's no hangover with it. I come home and cook. With my New England background there were never any red carpets, and I've always loved my work.

'I will go on working a little each year for the good of my soul, because I think to not keep working is death. Whether you are a film star or head of the Ford Motor Company, we must all keep working. I think working is the only salvation for your life.'

A few years later she was musing on reaching her mid seventies. 'I can't believe it,' she said, 'that I am the same age that my mother was when she died. She seemed so finished. I know that she just grew tired of life and decided to turn over and die. She told me so, and two weeks later she had gone. I am not ready to turn over yet.'

17

The Bette Davis Face

Bette was extremely lucky that not only did she have one of the greatest acting talents of all time, but she also had a fabulous face. It was to her advantage that she was not classically beautiful in the way that many of the other stars of her period were, because it allowed her to stand out from the crowd and to do some far more interesting work. She was not in the least vain about her appearance. She was perfectly willing to shave her head in order to play Elizabeth the First, and to look as old and ugly as necessary for *Baby Jane*. The part was what mattered, but the part she played most often, both in life and on the screen, was Bette Davis. For this major role she developed a very distinctive style. There were the eyes, and there was the mouth.

'Bette Davis Eyes' have become an institution. When I was still a young devotee, I used to talk to the songwriter Jackie de Shannon about them, and years later she wrote the song which Kim Carnes made famous, 'She's Got Bette Davis Eyes'. Bette was very pleased with the success of the song.

One day at Westport, when B.D. and her mother were sitting on the piano stool having one of their frequent head-to-head battles, Bette turned on her daughter with the angry words: 'Don't you give me that Bette Davis look!'

The eyes are often referred to as 'pop eyes' which they most certainly were not. They were large and they were expressive, and she was able to make them seem to 'pop' when she wanted to make a dramatic point. Her face, like her acting and her whole personality, was larger than life, and she worked to make it more so. Deciding, very early in her career, that her mouth was too small, she enlarged it by simply applying her lipstick over the lip-line. Over the years she became so adept at this that she could apply a full lipstick without even resorting to a mirror – she simply smeared on two scarlet slashes. She accentuated her eyes with some eyeliner, but again she could achieve the look in seconds. Whenever we were dressing to go out somewhere she could completely transform herself from the plain housebody to film star within a quarter of an hour. She just knew exactly what she was doing.

Bette was always very wary of the sun, since she had lost a layer of skin as a child, and burned very easily. The accident happened at school on a Christmas Eve. Bette was playing Santa Claus at a Christmas party and because there was no electricity the tree was decorated with candles. Bette was reaching down presents for the other children when she noticed that one of the candles had gone out. In relighting it, she set light to her sleeve and the whole costume burst into flames. Her face was severely blistered but with her mother's tireless ministrations she recovered, although the damaged skin added another dimension to the famous 'Bette Davis Look'.

For many years when I knew her, she objected to the idea of having a face-lift. She claimed that her face had done her very well so far, and there was no cause to change it. I could see no reason to contradict her, but as her seventieth birthday approached she began to think differently. She had water retention under the eyes and her neck was, not surprisingly, beginning to sag. I still believed that she didn't need to go under the knife but suggested that if she felt she had to, then a little tuck here and there was all that was necessary. She was still a very attractive woman who did not look her age.

In 1971 when she appeared at the National Film Theatre in London for her one-woman show, she wore 'lifts'. These are little pieces of tape which, when attached around the hairline, can 'lift' some sagging. During the reception afterwards she came up to me and whispered through gritted teeth: 'One of my lifts has gone.' I looked hard at her, but it was impossible to tell which it was.

She became more and more unhappy with the image she saw in the mirror and went to see a surgeon. He told her that she had, in all honesty, left it ten years too late. If he did anything at this late stage he could certainly make her look better for a few years, but by the time she was eighty she would definitely look it. He has been proved right. Bette was undecided about the operation for a long time and consulted other cosmetic surgeons, but finally went ahead with it as a seventieth birthday present to herself.

The chosen surgeon took pictures of her, scrubbed of make-up, just before he operated, and Bette made Peggy photograph her progress from the day the bandages came off. The 'before' pictures, which analysed her face, were necessarily stark. They are the cruellest pictures I have ever seen in my life. They show a death mask, robbed of the life and personality which made up Bette Davis. I was shocked by the sight of them. It is typical of Bette, however, that she wanted to record even this, the most grotesque period of her life. There was no vanity and no cover-up.

The operation left her desperately depressed. She was in a great deal of pain, and didn't believe she would ever recover. It was an immense operation for a woman of that age to endure, and some considerably younger women have even died from the shock of it. When I visited her in the Hollywood apartment she would be crushed by her misery. It was a terrible time, but as she healed I had to admit that the doctor had done a good job. She did look better, but it certainly wasn't enough of an improvement to have been worth so much agony.

For many months afterwards she wouldn't see anyone apart from close friends like myself, and nothing I could say would persuade her to start getting out and about again. Then she received a phone call from Sally Field, whom she didn't know at the time. Sally was having a romance with Burt Reynolds and she was organising a birthday party for him. She told Bette that she was Burt's favourite film star, and asked if she would come to the party. Bette decided that now was the time to come out of hiding, so she agreed.

Burt was standing by the bar in his home, opening a bottle of champagne when she arrived. He turned round and saw his idol walking into his house and did a classic double take, sending the bottle crashing to the ground. 'The face' was back in action. Bette enjoyed herself at the party, and Sally Field can take all the credit for having coaxed her out of her depression.

Bette's own hair is baby-fine and very pretty, but she did not always care for it as she should have done when she wasn't working, finding the chore boring. To save herself the trouble she asked Peggy Shannon to create some wigs for her. Peggy is one of the best in the business and she created some marvellous styles, one of which the rest of us referred to as 'her tiger wig' because it seemed the hair was striped. But to my eyes Bette always looked a hundred times better with her own hair brushed in the simple, Davis style.

One thing the Bette Davis face could be was intimidating. Bette knew this and used it to her advantage, terrorising young and nervous people with a grim stare. Many of B.D. and Jeremy's friends found the sight of B.D.'s mother glaring from the corner of a party or the kitchen more than their nerves could stand. One poor young man, stricken with terror, attempted to make light conversation with the living legend confronting him.

'Is it true, Miss Davis,' he asked, 'that when you first came to Hollywood it was said you had as much sex appeal as Slim Summerville?'

Slim Summerville was a gangling, one-toothed cowboy, and it was a well-known quote. Had Bette been a little kinder she would have laughed and admitted it. She was never, however, any good at laughing at herself and she turned on the unfortunate miscreant. B.D. had to hustle him from her presence and hide him in the billiard room until her mother had left.

When looking back at Bette's career the great face stands out in so many parts. In her greatest films it played as large a part in the creation of the characters as did her understanding of the lines. In *Now, Voyager!* she started the film with the face of a bushy-eyebrowed spinster aunt, and turned into the glamorous creature who could end the film with the immortal line: 'Why ask for the moon, we have the stars?'

The film is, of course, a classic, providing a wish-fulfilment fantasy for millions of women during the austere war years. It showed that no matter how plain or dowdy a girl was, it only required the right attentions from the right men, in this case medical as well as romantic, to turn her into a glamorous heroine. They too, it said, could become Bette Davis.

Probably her most famous portrayal was that of Margot Channing in *All About Eve*. The part was originally to be played by Gertrude Lawrence, but she disagreed with the director because she wanted to sing a song and he wouldn't allow it, and she stormed out. Claudette Colbert was then cast, but withdrew because of a back ailment, giving Bette the part which probably marked the peak of her career.

Margot Channing was going to be forty-five, but director/writer Joseph Mankiewicz reduced it to forty for Bette. In his biography of Bette, Charles Higham quotes Mankiewicz:

> Forty years of age. Four O. Give or take a year the single most critical chronological milestone in the life of an actress. Look, I knew these women. I'd been in love with some – I'd worked with many of them. In the early 1930s I'd watch them roll into Paramount and Metro at six thirty in the morning on their way to hairdressing and make-up. Drive in usually with the top down, their hair all blown in the wind, no lipstick, their own eyelashes, wearing anything from a poncho to a polo coat – and I'd think Perc Westmore (the make-up man), should be arrested for so much as touching a powder puff to their loveliness. Well, by the late thirties they were driving with the top up. Then in the forties they started wearing scarves, and by 1950 large hats. The pancake was getting thicker, the make-up took longer, the cameramen started using specially-built little banks of 'inkies' to iron out wee bags and sags.

As with so many of her parts, Bette became associated with Margot Channing in the minds of her fans. The witty, bitchy, hard-drinking, hard-smoking, hard-living actress seemed to be Bette. She often used to say to me, 'Why don't the fans ever want pictures of me in *The Catered Affair*, why does it always have to be *All About Eve*?' The reason was simple. In *The Catered Affair*, she was in character, which was what Bette liked to do best, in *Eve* she was appearing with 'The Bette Davis Face', and that is what the fans wanted to treasure and remember.

The story was based on the actress Elisabeth Bergner, who was appearing in *The Two Mrs Carrolls* on Broadway during the Second World War when a young actress playing a small part came to her to say she would be quitting. Miss Bergner asked 'Why?' And the young actress said, 'Because I'm not good enough, not good enough to be with you. You're so magnificent!' Bergner persuaded the young actress to stay on. Her name was Irene Worth and she grew into a star herself. The difference was that Bergner and Worth remained friends. This was the basis for the story of *All About Eve* but, of course, without the sense of evil which pervades the film.

Bette has never shown any vanity about her face. When she had the facelift it was purely for professional reasons, to get more work. Her face interests her, as a tool of her trade, but she was always convinced that she was plain, and never worried about how she looked on screen, as long as it was 'in character'. Even when she first arrived in Hollywood in the 1930s, when glamour seemed to be the most important ingredient in every actress's career, she wanted to get away from it. In *Fashions of 1934* she allowed the studio to turn her into a typical Hollywood starlet, but it was just another part to her, not a career move. In the same year she won the role of Mildred, the bitter, cruel waitress who taunts the crippled London intellectual in Somerset Maugham's book *Of Human Bondage*. The director of the movie, John Cromwell, explained later why he cast Bette.

The first day I met Bette Davis I knew she had to be Mildred. What struck me most about her? Her courage. No other actress in Hollywood would have dared face a camera with her hair untidy and badly rinsed, her clothes cheap and tawdry, her manner vicious and ugly. She worked like a dog on her cockney accent, she made you feel she had been on her feet all day and much of the night as well, serving food: the most exhausting of jobs for a woman, and the most humiliating.

She said to me, 'A girl like Mildred must look ill; she has tuberculosis and she's poor.' I told her to do her own make-up any way she wanted so long as she didn't overdo it. After all, Mildred couldn't have been literally dying, she had to have the energy of pure evil. I sensed a desperation in Davis. It wasn't just the desperation of an unhappy woman whose marriage was going wrong. She was frightened, really frightened that the worst thing of all would happen to her as an actress: that she would become bored with her work, that she would develop a block and lose her career. Mildred was her chance, once and for all, to make the big time. And yet I never felt she was overdoing it. My faith in her was supported by the knowledge that her greatness would be tempered by discipline.

18

Bette and Me

Although I was a devoted admirer of Bette Davis the film star, the way in which I valued her most was as a friend. When she decided that she couldn't marry me to help me obtain my green card to live and work in the USA, she went to enormous trouble to write a letter on my behalf to the immigration authorities, vouching for my character and assuring them I would make a worthy American citizen. She was always very interested in everything that happened in my life, and encouraged me to move to America where she was sure I could be more successful – an opinion which in time has been proved correct. When I wrote a screenplay with Jerry Kass (of *Ballroom* fame) for her, which she decided she was too old to play in, she wrote personally to Elizabeth Taylor on my behalf asking her to 'read it for her friend Roy Moseley'.

She could always be trusted to deliver whatever she promised, and disliked it if you reminded her of something she had said she would do. I was very keen to get an interview with Steve McQueen, and she said she would fix it for me. A few days later I made the mistake of reminding her of her promise. She was furious.

'Why do you keep asking me? I told you I would do it, and I will do it.'

As it turned out even she couldn't achieve this promise for me since Steve explained to her that he was not seeing anybody at that time.

The kindness which she showed to my parents and to me was wonderful, and I tried to repay it in every way I could. Sometimes it was better that she didn't even know what I was doing for her. When she rang from America to tell me she was coming over to England to film and wanted to stay in rooms at one of her favourite restaurants, The Compleat Angler in Marlow, which was also a small hotel, I said I would arrange it. I went to the restaurant to look at the rooms they had to offer. They were very beautiful, but I just knew they were going to be wrong for Bette. She need more privacy and more space. I rang her back to say that I didn't think this was the best choice, but she was adamant. There was nothing I could do to dissuade her, but I knew that within about three days of arriving there she would want to leave. I contacted a famous estate agent in Ascot and explained my problem.

'I need a house, but I can't guarantee that I will take it,' I explained. He was a good friend of mine and agreed to find a house in Ascot and hold onto it as long as possible.

When Bette and Vik arrived in England I explained the situation to Vik, and he said he would take care of his end. Sure enough, within a few days she wanted out and Vik called me. I was able to arrange for her to go to the house in Ascot, which she loved, without ever having to admit that I had set the whole thing up. I always felt safe in organising anything for Bette, because I always knew how she would react.

When I met Lucille Ball she told me that she had been at the same acting school as Bette. Lucy had been a 'new girl' just as Bette was leaving, and she remembered seeing Bette on stage and thinking, 'That girl is going to be a star'.

When I next saw Bette I told her that I believed she had been to school with Lucy.

'No.' Bette shook her head.

'You must have been, Bette,' I insisted, 'she said so.'

'I don't remember her!' Bette flared.

Soon afterwards Bette was appearing in her one-woman show at Long Beach, California, and one of the first questions from a member of the audience was, 'Is that Lucille Ball in the third row?'

Bette shaded her eyes from the lights and called out into the audience: 'Is that you Lucy? Are you there?'

'Yes, Bette,' Lucy called back.

'We go back a long way, don't we, Lucy? We went to acting school together, didn't we?'

'Yes, we did!' shouted the delighted Lucy. Bette had decided to hedge her bets and trust that my information was correct.

After the show I took my great friend Gavin Kern backstage and Lucy was also there. I noticed that Gavin wasn't circulating and I went over and offered to introduce him around.

'Don't worry about me, Roy,' he said. 'I'm quite happy to stand here in a corner and just watch the two biggest women in our profession operating in the same room.' I have to add that Gavin was not only a very well-known Hollywood agent, but one of the best-looking men in town – quite a compliment to the two 'girls'.

Bette later told me she didn't much like Lucy – perhaps it was rather too much competition.

At the bottom of the garden of the house in Ascot was a little cottage, which at that time had been rented by the actress Liv Ullman. Miss Ullman was most keen to meet Bette and was forever staring out of the windows and rushing outside when she saw Bette going down to the vegetable garden, which backed on to the cottage. Rather ungraciously, Bette kept her back turned on the poor woman, refusing to acknowledge her existence.

'Every time I go out this woman is peering out the window at me,' she said, 'so I show her my ass.'

On the last day of her stay, however, her telephone went out of order and she was forced to go down to Miss Ullman and ask if she could use hers. Miss Ullman consequently got a whole morning of Bette Davis to herself, and the two of them got on very well.

Bette's sixtieth birthday fell during the filming of *Connecting Rooms* and she was being plagued with requests from the media for interviews which she really didn't have time to give. She asked me to arrange a party for her somewhere private, to which she could invite all the relevant journalists and, as their hostess, could spend time with each of them. I suggested Inigo Jones restaurant in Covent Garden which was very fashionable at that time, and she gave me a budget of £300 for the event, which would be more like £3,000 today. However, the management of the restaurant, whom I knew personally, were so keen to have Bette that they negotiated a ridiculously small fee.

We hired the restaurant from six to nine p.m., and sat everyone down very informally in little groups at separate tables to eat, after a happy cocktail hour at which hot snacks were provided. There were hors d'oeuvres, entrées, desserts, coffee and liqueurs. Sir Michael Redgrave was also there. Bette moved around the room like a perfect hostess, giving everyone exactly the material they needed. On the dot of nine she stood up and said, 'Ladies and gentlemen, goodnight,' and swept out to her waiting white Rolls Royce. The gates came down on the bar and the party was over.

She was the consummate professional. I was happy at the great success of the evening, and most relieved when it was over.

When Gladys Cooper, who had appeared with Bette in *Now, Voyager!*, died in England, Bette asked me to order a wreath and arrange for it to be delivered. She used me continually like that, and I was always happy to do anything I could for her.

I was always an unfailing champion for Bette when she wasn't there to protect her own interests. When *Connecting Rooms* came out it was unable to obtain a proper release, so a special showing was arranged at the Mayfair Hotel. I was invited to represent Bette, since she was in America. During the showing Sir Michael Redgrave was given some Belgian Award for 'Best Actor', and the director received another award. Neither of them gave Bette Davis any mention in their speeches. I was furious and pointedly left the modest festivities. When the director 'phoned to find out why I had left early I told him how furious I was, and what an injustice I felt they had done to Bette, without whom there wouldn't have been a film.

One of the most rewarding moments I can remember during our fifteen years together, was when I realised that she was so used to having me around she hardly noticed me. It happened when she was rehearsing on the set one day. I arrived and stood watching for a while. As always she was completely absorbed in her character. I noticed her take out a cigarette and I went over to light it – which is something most actresses hate to have done for them. She took the light but said nothing and went on working. Exactly twenty minutes later she took out another cigarette and I lit it again. She looked up.

'Hi, darling,' she exclaimed, 'when did you arrive?' She was totally unaware of my having lit the first cigarette for her.

However discreet you are, there is always talk about a friendship like mine and Bette's. My picture would appear in the background on news shots of her arriving at airports. Friends (and foes) gradually realised that I did indeed know Bette Davis. One does not talk too much about friendship with one so well-known because there is a certain amount of foolish jealousy – but more importantly, out of respect to Bette. I don't think she would have appreciated my broadcasting my friendship with her to all and sundry.

However, friends soon started to ask me what Bette Davis was actually like, what did we talk about, and all the other questions that people have about a great lady. At dinner parties, if the atmosphere was right, I would develop a little cabaret routine, using Bette's voice to tell funny stories about what had happened to us, or what we had talked about. It always went down very well, and nothing personal was ever mentioned.

One evening I was invited to a dinner by my good friend, film producer Bruce Cohn Curtis. It was to raise some money and so it was important that everything went well. He had told me that I must do my Bette Davis routine after dinner, and I must give it all I had to amuse his guests. Everyone loved Bette Davis. I planned exactly what I would do. I went through my usual routine and then, at the end, I picked up the 'phone, still using Bette's voice. I pointed to an extension phone and said, 'Bruce, pick that up, the rest of you line up behind.'

Then I dialled Bette's number at the hotel in Albuquerque, New Mexico, where she was staying while working on location with Ernest Borgnine in *Bunny O'Hare*. As Bette's voice came on the line I chatted away to her, making sure that we stayed on strictly neutral ground, while all the dinner guests took turns at listening to the 'real thing'. It was a bit naughty, but it was a real showstopper.

When we were together we talked all the time. There were never any silences or gaps, no moments when either of us thought, 'What are we going to talk about now?' Sometimes she would shout at me, sometimes I would flare up at her – quietly! – like any two people who spend a lot of time together, but I could easily parry anything she threw at me. She would get things into her mind and she would have to stage a little drama. You just had to keep calm and wait for the storm to pass, and then you could reason with her again. When we were alone she was always totally adorable and delightful.

One year I was in New York with Christian Roberts and we were both due to go down to Twin Bridges for the weekend. When I rang Bette she said firmly, 'Come alone.' I was embarrassed, but I suggested to Christian that I would go down on the Saturday and he could follow for lunch on Sunday. All through Saturday she griped about Christian coming, saying that she wanted us to be alone. On Sunday morning I said, 'Okay Bette, I'd better ring Christian and put him off.'

'No,' she stopped me. 'I know you want Christian to come, so invite him for dinner.' I was relieved and apprehensive at the same time, but I did as she suggested.

Later she said to me, 'I know you want to go and meet him, so take the car.'

When I picked Christian up at the station I warned him that Bette might be in a funny mood, and that he must not think it was anything to do with him if we had a 'bumpy night'. Bette, however, had set her mind on being lovely, and it was one of the nicest visits ever. We talked long into the evening and both stayed at the house overnight. She told Christian that she had recently seen *The Anniversary*, which they had made together, on television and, although she had not thought much of his performance at the time, she now thought it was 'very good'. It was generous praise from such a star to a relative newcomer, and it was equally generous of her to invite him to her home, not only as my friend but in his own right as a British film star. She showed me so many kindnesses in so many ways that they more than made up for the difficult times.

She liked the way I treated her. She liked to be respected and treated as a lady; she liked good manners. She liked going out with me. She said we 'looked good together', although we seldom went anywhere where we would be seen by the general public. She liked to be with someone who had experienced life, but who didn't crave to be seen with Bette Davis. Obviously I always enjoyed being seen with her, but I was just as happy to stay at home, just the two of us. I had been to the best restaurants and stayed in the best hotels. I didn't need to use her as a ticket to the good life, and she appreciated and knew my feelings for her and her company.

The most important thing to me was that she should like my mother, who has always been the most important person in my life, and she did, unreservedly. She said that she knew if we ever got married she wouldn't have 'mother-in-law trouble'.

Many of my friends were astonished by the friendship. I think in the beginning they believed I was romancing. It was the greatest romance imaginable for me. When we first met, Bette gave me a picture of herself and wrote across it: 'Oh Roy, how can I ever live up to what you think of me?' But she did, and surpassed herself, in so many ways.

I learned so much from her, just by watching and listening. There is now a lot of her in me, in the way I talk when doing my business deals. I remember the way she played with words was wonderful, the way she emphasised different words for impact, to create that magical delivery. It was pure genius and I have learned many lessons from it.

Bette showed great kindness to people who wrote to her with their problems. An actor called Jay Robinson had fallen on hard times and wrote to Bette for help. She found him a part in a film and helped him to get his career back into shape. Nancy Kulp, who became famous as the hard-faced banker's secretary in the *Beverly Hillbillies*, also wrote about her problems and the two actresses fell into a long correspondence.

When a young Debbie Reynolds confessed that she was nervous about working with her, Bette gave her a piece of advice.

'Never be afraid of the Greats,' she said. 'Always work with the Greats. They will make you great!'

I have followed that advice all my life, and have never had cause to regret it.

19

The End of a Beautiful Friendship

Sooner or later Bette managed to alienate everyone in her life, even those dearest to her. She did it to her family, to her friends and her servants. The first was her sister Bobby, who worked as Bette's 'servant' for many years and, if B.D. is to be believed, received nothing but unpleasantness in return. She was the one member of the family I never met during my friendship with Bette. Towards the end, when Bette was in Hollywood, she received news that Bobby, who then lived in Phoenix, Arizona, was dying of cancer. I asked Bette if she planned to visit her sister one more time.

'If Bobby wants to see me she can come here, even if she has to crawl,' was the shockingly heartless reply. 'I'm not dragging myself over to Phoenix to see her.'

It seemed that despite her great fame and great professional success, she never believed that she was given the love and respect which was her due. She perpetually demanded more and more attention. Peggy Shannon would have made a marvellous companion for her in her old age, but Peggy's health was not good after a back accident, and Bette had to have someone with her all the time. I think also that Peggy finally tired of being treated badly by someone who should have been her friend.

Vik would also have been an enormous help to her in the last years, and I believe that she did put out feelers to see if he could be coaxed back, but he told me that he had had enough and was no longer willing to put up with all the inevitable trouble.

Bette always preferred to have a male secretary, but she couldn't find anyone who would stay with her. At one stage she managed to persuade Taylor Pero to take the job. Taylor had started in the business as a dancer with Johnny Mathis, and had become well-known as Lana Turner's secretary. When Bette offered him the job he couldn't resist the temptation, but he left after four days.

'I had always wanted to meet her,' he told me later, 'and it was very interesting, but there would have been no way I could have continued working for such a woman.' Considering how long he had been with Lana, who was also not an easy woman to get on with, this shows how difficult Bette was becoming.

She had to dominate everyone around her, and yet she despised anyone whom she was able to dominate. The people who stood up to her, like B.D., were constantly put to the test and challenged to love her more.

From the first time I saw her ripping the pages out of her Rollerdex, fifteen years earlier, I had known that my time would come as well, and I actually did remarkably well to last as long as I did. Hardly anyone else could claim such a record. I think I lasted because she liked me as a person, but also felt happy that I was a great admirer of her work. I believed she was the greatest of film actresses, and one of the great personalities of the century. Bette was not a conceited woman, but she was proud of her achievements. At the same time I was strong enough not to allow her to walk all over me. I maintained my own separate life, and she must have known that if she upset me I could just stop seeing her without my world falling to pieces. I offered her no sort of competition professionally, and when I was with her I was prepared to be entirely at her beck and call. At the same time she knew that, like her, I was a fighter, someone for whom nothing had been easily won.

As everyone else began to disappear around me, however, I knew that my time in her favour was limited. First of all Vik went, then the delightful Peggy Shannon chose to drift away. Bette had enormous trouble finding anyone to do anything for her. Her tyranny over servants was horrible to behold, and none of them would stay for long. She eventually found a young girl called Kathryn Sermak from San Bernadino to be her secretary and companion.

Kathryn was a pleasant-looking girl, who knew nothing about the film industry, Hollywood or the great legend whom she was coming to serve. I didn't know if this would work or not. Something about her made me uneasy from the first meeting; I found her hard and unapproachable, and disliked her from the first time we met. Why, I wondered, should I feel this way about a young Californian girl? It didn't seem to make sense.

When I first met Kathryn, she was staying with Bette at the Berystede Hotel. Bette rang me, 'I've booked you a room here, Roy,' she said. 'Come for the weekend.'

On the Saturday night Bette and I had dinner together on our own. I got the impression that this did not please Kathryn, but she didn't make an issue of it. On the Sunday morning Bette didn't feel like putting her face on and asked me if I would mind taking Kathryn down for brunch, and bringing her back something on a plate to eat in her suite. I minded very much but I obeyed dutifully.

Kathryn and I started to talk to one another. She chatted about politics for a while, and then I changed the subject. I tried to explain to her just what an opportunity she was being offered.

'What a wonderful opportunity this job is for you, Kathryn,' I said. 'Bette Davis is the greatest film star ever, you will be able to learn so much. Study the way she works. When she is filming, for instance, you will see that from the moment she gets up in the morning she is concentrating completely on her work. She is the consummate professional. You will be able to see why she is so brilliant. And when you get to the studios and see the other actors and actresses, you will be able to see why they have not reached Bette's supreme success, and why there are only a small number of artists in this lady's league.'

We chatted for a while, and I thought that we seemed to be communicating fairly well. That night, after dinner, I went home. The 'phone was ringing as I came in through the front door.

'How dare you!' she exploded.

'How dare I what, Bette?'

'How dare you ask Kathryn about what I'm like first thing in the morning?'

'Bette,' I said, 'I've seen you more times than Kathryn in the morning. Why would I ask her anything like that?'

'No!' she said, 'I have to take Kathryn's word.'

She ranted and raved about this invasion of privacy for a while, and although I explained what it was that I had actually said, she wouldn't accept my explanation. Once she had hung up, however, she must have thought about it all more calmly, because a few days later I received a letter.

Some years before I had asked Lord Mountbatten to inscribe a copy of his book to Bette. It is not something that members of the royal family like to do, but he agreed to do it for Bette. Now another book had been published about him and I had offered to get her a copy. I went to Hatchards in Piccadilly and had it sent, unsigned, to the hotel.

Bette's letter thanked me for the book. 'As to my phone call' she wrote, 'I should have skipped it! Catherine [sic] is apt to misunderstand, as she is in a way insecure, and if she thinks she is being used – as she is a very loyal person to whomever she works for – is too apt to jump to conclusions.' Bette seemed to have learned much about her employee in a very short time – or had she? She ended the letter cordially, hoping to see me again soon, but from this point on the relationship between Bette and the rest of us became more and more distant, to the point that there seemed to be a solid wall between her and us. Finally it seems no-one, not even B.D., was able to breach her defences.

I had made it very clear how strongly I disliked Kathryn. I indicated to Bette that I did not want to have anything further to do with her, and Bette seemed to understand. When I visited her, Kathryn was mostly out of sight.

At this time my great friend, Charles Higham, was writing a biography of Bette. She was not happy at the prospect, having had complete control over the two previous books about her life, with the result that they didn't reveal anything that couldn't be found in any fan magazine. I greatly feared that the publication of the book would be the last straw for our friendship. She would need someone to blame and she was aware that I knew Charles. Charles most generously said that if I could win Bette's agreement, I could co-author the book with him. I suggested the idea to her, explaining that it would mean she would have access to the manuscript.

'Certainly not,' she replied. 'If he writes it I'll sue him.'

The book came out and in the flyleaf of my copy Charles wrote an inscription:

Roy,
My good, good friend. This is the one book you had nothing to do with. Looking forward to books you will have lots to do with. Fondest regards,
Charles.

179

I knew things were going wrong when I went to see Bette at the Lombardy Hotel in New York at Christmas time. I was staying at another hotel, the Shoreham, just a few blocks away from the Lombardy. I had just written my book *A Life with the Stars* and I wanted to ask her to write a foreword for me. I also wanted to make sure that she didn't harbour any grudges against me regarding Charles's biography of her, which had by then been published for over two months.

When I arrived in the room there had been some sort of accident in which Kathryn had broken a screen. I exchanged a formal courtesy with her and she melted into the background. I sat down with Bette, and we began to talk about Charles's book, which Bette claimed she hadn't read.

'I suspected you of helping Higham with his book,' she said.

'Did you, Bette?'

'Yes, but there are forty-eight reasons why I know that you didn't. Forty-eight things that you know about me which aren't mentioned in the book.'

'I thought you hadn't read it.'

'B.D. read it,' she covered quickly, but I was sure she was lying.

'Bette,' I said, 'I have to tell you, Charles has agreed to co-author a book on Merle Oberon with me. In fact I am about to leave for California to begin work on it. This is a professional engagement, and it's a big chance for me. It's like you being offered a film with a co-star I don't like.'

'Of course.' She was all reasonableness. 'I have always wished you the best. When you are in California we will be able to see each other.'

'I would also like to ask you to write a foreword to my book *A Life with the Stars*,' I went on. She nodded and took out a pen.

'Roy,' she wrote, 'you have known us all so well. Why not write a book? I look forward to reading it – Love Bette.'

I hadn't received my usual Christmas card and I asked if she had sent it, worried that it might have got lost. She seemed flustered, pretended that it must have got mislaid, and pulled out another one for me. She also gave me a new picture which she had had taken and inscribed it, ominously, 'For Roy, one photo more – My love Bette.'

By now I could see that Bette was growing old, but she was still a 'gutsy dame', full of fighting spirit and still good-looking. She should have been mellowing and enjoying the fruits of her long run of success, but she wasn't. The bullying, 'monster' side of her nature had not abated; if anything it had grown worse. She should have been able to lead the life of a happy, if rather spoiled old lady, but I feared she would end up a sad, bad, lonely old 'monster'.

In Hollywood a couple of weeks later I received an hysterical call from her, ordering me to have nothing more to do with Charles. I again explained that I was now a writer and that Charles was a professional colleague of mine. She was not, however, willing to let the case rest. There is no doubt that someone else had contributed to this level of anger where she was determined to rid herself of me.

'Any friend of Charles Higham's cannot be a friend of mine,' she hissed angrily.

I remained very calm. 'Who is, Bette?' I asked quietly. 'Who is?' I replaced the receiver gently before she had time to hang up on me. The first emotion which I felt was a wave of relief.

From that moment on nothing seemed to go right for Bette. First she was diagnosed as having cancer and had to have a mastectomy. This led to her having a stroke. Bette did not take easily to being a patient. Vik's sister Stephanie, who is a nurse, visited her frequently and reported that her behaviour was impossible. Then, when she finally returned home, she fell and broke her hip. But the 'gutsy Yankee Dame' survived it all.

The worst blow of all must have been the publication of B.D.'s book, *My Mother's Keeper*. When I first heard that the book had been written, I couldn't believe it. I never would have thought that B.D. and Jeremy would have done such a thing. The things they said were quite horrible, and the act of betrayal far worse than Christina Crawford's of Joan. For one thing B.D. was actually Bette's real daughter; also, at least Christina waited until Joan was dead before publishing. There is no doubt that Bette drove B.D. hard, but she had always been like that. For years Jeremy and B.D. had coped with their tremendous mother-in-law problem. However bad it might have been, and at times it was terrible, they did not give up. But finally B.D. found all possible lines of communication with her mother had been blocked. She had to do something to let Bette know how she felt, and this was the only way she could think of.

Naturally Bette was mortified, but instead of seeing it as just one more battle in the long-running war which she always seemed to relish fighting, she decided to withdraw from the fray completely and to 'adopt' Kathryn as her surrogate daughter. She certainly gave Kathryn a hard time as well, but Kathryn must have decided that it was worth the suffering for the reward of becoming indispensable to her employer. It wasn't hard for her to do, since Bette had chased everyone else away. When Kathryn went away to Paris, Bette was unable to find even a temporary replacement, and Kathryn was able to return on her own terms.

New responsibilities came her way. Not only was she the surrogate daughter, she became the surrogate manager and even executive producer on Bette's last film *The Wicked Stepmother*. However, producer or not, Kathryn lost her star early in the production – Bette walked out of the film and, it seemed finally, out of her long and fabulous career. Who now would risk this behaviour again?

I sometimes see Bette on chat shows promoting her book, or talking about her illnesses and operations, and I imagine what her life must be like now, locked in that lonely apartment in West Hollywood, full of hate, resentment and unhappiness, and with her health failing. She hasn't lost her spirit, and still comes out to work when she can, but the offers are becoming fewer as her reputation gets worse.

Directly after her recovery from her illness, she came to England to make an 'all-star' Agatha Christie film with Sir John Mills, who she had always admired and wanted to work with. Sir John and the rest of the cast were all horrified by her behaviour, particularly towards the equally distinguished Helen Hayes, and Bette had to be moved out of the hotel where the rest of the company was staying and into the Savoy. If you view the film now you will see shots in which the whole cast are assembled – with one notable exception. It must have been easier to shoot round her rather than put up with her.

The film *Whales of August* (1986) was a great personal triumph for her, showing that she had fought her illnesses and come out on top once again, but the producers and director of the film did not find working with her a happy experience. Her co-star was Lillian Gish, who was ten years older than Bette, with a distinguished and long career behind her. Miss Gish had trouble remembering her lines, and needed to have them fed to her by the director. Bette would cruelly draw attention to this, calling out, 'Leave her alone, let her do it her way.'

The crew threw a birthday party for Miss Gish. As they were cutting the cake a harsh voice shouted out from the back. 'Go on, Lillian, tell them how old you really are.'

The difficulties between the two stars became well known. When Bette appeared on the Carson show, Johnny Carson asked her about their relationship and the audience laughed. Bette turned on them savagely, accusing them of mocking Miss Gish and jumping to her colleague's defence. Johnny Carson tried to defuse the situation by asking her which co-stars she hadn't liked, and she went into a familiar tirade against Faye Dunaway.

Lillian Gish, who is a lady – something that Bette most definitely is not – finally spoke out in an interview. 'I look at that sad face,' she said, 'and I just feel so terribly sorry for that woman.'

She is quite right: it is all in the face, just as it always has been. The face shows a broken, twisted woman. She has finally become an ugly woman, something which she always thought she was. When I see this unpleasant person on the screen, it is hard to look back on that wonderful lady I once knew.

I would have been pleased to have been with her. With me around her, I think her health could have been a little better, and she would not now be quite the frail wreck which she seems to have become. But Bette, throughout her life, deliberately chose the hardest furrows to plough, both professionally and personally. It does not detract from the legend, and perhaps even adds to it.

Bette and I were to see each other again after the split, but only across a crowded room. It was during an AFI Tribute to the director Frank Capra. Bette was sitting at the top table and behaving abominably. Mrs Capra was dying of emphysema, and was seated close to an oxygen cylinder. Bette was asked not to smoke and made a great fuss about it, continually leaving the table during the ceremony to go outside for a cigarette. Nobody had a good word to say about her that evening, and she received only a muted welcome from the audience. The mad, bad, sad, lonely old lady had come out of her lair, and people did not like what they saw. To Bette's horror Claudette Colbert, making her first personal appearance in many years to applaud Mr Capra, took the evening by the scruff of the neck.

During a break in the proceedings I went to the table and

slipped a note into Bette's napkin. It said: 'Bette, You know I'm not to blame.'

I often think about her in that flat, and feel sad. I have met people who have been to see her and they all tell me the same story. They go once, or perhaps twice, and Bette is so unpleasant to them that they never want to go back. I am tempted to call her, but I know that I would not be allowed to speak to her since even B.D.'s calls are not put through. I miss her friendship, her laughter, her affection, and yes, I miss Bette Davis. She was one hell of a dame. She was helpful to me in so many ways. She gave me so much. Above all, she gave me her name, and helped me in this most difficult profession, a profession where she was the undisputed queen.

On one of her visits to England I asked her if she would like to meet the Queen. 'Why should I?' she replied. 'I am a queen.'

As this book is a memoir, I have no acknowledgements to make. However, it would not have seen the light of day without the faith and support of these important people who rescued my work and helped me to bring it to life.

In alphabetical order they are:

Mitch Douglas
Charles Higham
Karen Hurrell
Gillian Paul
Victoria Shellin
Robert Smith

– and, of course,
Bette Davis.

Index